The revelation given in the Value Exch̶ ̶ ̶ ̶ ̶ ̶ ̶the hands of those who minister to set th̶ ̶ ̶ ̶ ̶ embraces the intimacy of relationship that ̶ ̶ ̶ it is equipping in its purpose to help peopl̶ ̶ ̶ ̶ ̶ ̶ ̶ ̶ ̶ ̶ ̶ ̶ our own steps to freedom with Holy Spirit anywhere a̶̶ ̶ ̶̶ ̶ ̶y̶ ̶ time. This biblical approach to making the exchanges that Jesus provides deals with issue of life in our present circumstances or even with things that have plagued our soul for decades. It is a tool that empowers new levels of authority, confidence, and victory to be attained in the simplest way I've ever experienced healing and freedom could be. It has changed the way I lead people in steps of healing and freedom, that cause them to look to Jesus ONLY as their healer, their Savior and deliverer.

SHANNA M. NEAL
Co-Senior Pastor of Christian Life Center, South Bend

I am thankful for the Value Exchange method of healing. It changed my life! I struggled with anxiety and depression for most of my adulthood. I was introduced to the tool by a dear friend and mentor. At first, I was a bit apprehensive. But the more I pursued healing, the stronger and healthier I became. The Value Exchange enhanced my ability to hear God's voice and gain perspective about His love for me and open my heart to receive healing. This has empowered me to live in the fullness of His promise!

JOAN MCCLENDON M. MIN and MATS
Coauthor, *Life on the Fringe: Testimonies of Women Moving Beyond Desperation to Faith*

After being diagnosed with stage 4 cancer, I became overwhelmed with anxiety and fear. I was introduced to the Value Exchange. I was led through the process at a pace that was comfortable for me. As I worked through the steps, I experienced God's healing power. A heavy weight was lifted from my shoulders. I am forever grateful.

MIKE OVERPECK
Pastor, Co-founder of One Community Faith and Family

The Value Exchange is a pathway to wholeness I've been hoping to find for years to address my personal hurts and wounds. It has become a priceless tool in our ministry as we help individuals and couples restore and repair relationships. We thank God for this tool that brings healing to a broken world.

TARA OVERPECK
Co-founder of One Community Faith and Family

As a lay counselor I have received various forms of inner healing/deliverance training, attended seminars, read countless books, and listened to numerous podcasts, YouTube clips and sermons that have empowered me in my ministry to hurting women. While I have many tools in my ministry toolbox, none has been as streamlined and effective as The Value Exchange. I tend to shy away from formulaic ministry approaches; however, I have found that the Value Exchange offers such flexibility that is has become a multi-use tool. No matter the depth of a person's strongholds or wounding, this has been my go-to instrument for healing. As I primarily work with women in addiction, I find this approach directly addresses breaking the power of addiction, idolatry, and self-sabotage. It aids in breaking the power of ungodly soul ties and generational curses/sin patterns. The Value Exchange is especially helpful in working through incapacitating trauma while not revisiting the paralyzing events until after healing has taken place.

I always tell the women I sit with that my goal is to work myself out of a job by empowering and teaching them this tool so they can apply it personally and share it with others. It has become the gift that keeps on giving. It must also be stated that before I began to utilize this concept in ministry, I first applied it to myself and have found deep freedom and healing as a result. Intimate struggles that I assumed were my "thorn in the flesh" have been dismissed as I came out of agreement with powerlessness, shame, and rejection. As God continues to refine me, I am brought to repentance and freedom every time I revisit these principles.

I am deeply grateful for the time taken to put these concepts into written format for others to utilize in their personal lives as well as in ministry.

KATI SCHMUCKER
Director of Biblical Counseling at SPA Women's
Ministry Homes, Inc.

What do I do:

When a knot in my stomach rises to a lump in my throat? When tension turns into a pain in the neck and tightness across my shoulders? When irritation erupts in temper ready to snap like a turtle, pull into a shell and hang out a "no visitors" sign?

I go to the Value Exchange class with Londa and Dr. Rachelle! They have helped me to identify the emotion behind the tension and to define what purpose it serves, and do I want to choose to be free of it.

Do I want Freedom!?? YES! They have opened so many doors to freedom for me to walk through to relief. How do I spell relief?

V A L U E   E X C H A N G E. It works. Better than sitting by a fire drinking hot chocolate on a zero-degree January day. Each event leaves me with a *happy ever after* when I recall the reward I received in the Exchange. I'm looking forward to moving on to more freedom and am so grateful for this training.

CAROL WIELAND
Goshen, Indiana

I am so grateful for Londa and Rachelle and all the love and compassion for people that has compelled their ministry and inspired the writing of this book. This book was written with prayer and perseverance, tears and triumph—with many Value Exchanges for their own personal struggles in writing the book and with the relentless pursuit of excellence, in order to put this book into our hands. This book is a treasure trove filled with wisdom, experiential knowledge and hands-on help for those seeking greater freedom emotionally and physically through Christian inner healing. Knowing both Londa and Rachelle, I can say unequivocally that this book is tested, tried, and true! They have many years of experience between the two of them doing Value Exchanges on themselves, many hours of using it to bring freedom to others, along with teaching and equipping the body of Christ to use these tools for themselves and with others. So get ready to board the "Freedom Express" and look for greater healing to manifest as you read and use the tools in this book.

MAGGIE JUDD
Goshen, Indiana

As far as I could remember the Lord put a desire in my heart to know Him and be close to Him. However, through life's experience unknowingly I began to view Father as the Godfather instead of Father God. The enemy had convinced me I had to earn God's love. Ironically, I had no idea these were subtle seeds of deception that I just believed to be true. The worst part about this is I could read and talk about the Love of God, but had an underlying belief system that was robbing me from the greatest love in all creation. The Value Exchange has allowed Holy Spirit to peel back layers of lies I had accepted as truth, having no idea they were there. Jeremiah 17:19 - I now can live in a place of truth and occupy a space with the Lord with no disconnect. Thank you, Father, for paying my debt forever and allowing me to grow in your Love. Nothing compares to the intimacy with the Lord!

RICH MASSON
President, Wave Express Goshen, Indiana

The Value Exchange has allowed me the privilege of seeing many people encounter the love of God and access healing that has evaded them by other means. Londa's approach is simple but powerful, making room for Holy Spirit to work. Because of its simplicity, I've used Value Exchange not just in counseling sessions, but also in altar ministry, in conversations with friends and with my children. As a worship leader, I have led entire congregations to God's healing using Value Exchange. But the gift that I have been the most grateful for is that I can sit in a room alone with the Lord and seek healing through the Value Exchange for myself. This has catapulted my intimacy with God. I had no concept of living life free until Londa introduced me to what was possible. It gives me great joy to see this manual published and placed in willing hands. To God be the glory!

MARKETO CHRISTINE MICHEL
Worship Pastor, That Church Downtown, South Bend, Indiana

the Value Exchange

the Value Exchange

A Practical, Supernatural Way to Finally Free Yourself from Wounded Thinking

THE DEFINITIVE GUIDE

LONDA **HARWELL** RACHELLE **CROWDER, M.D.**

Value Exchange: A Practical, Supernatural Way to
Finally Free Yourself from Wounded Thinking

Londa Harwell, Rachelle Crowder, M.D.

ISBN-13: 978-0-578-38501-3
Library of Congress Control Number: 2022904129

Freedom Express Ministries™
FreedomExpress16.org

This book is manufactured in the United States of America.

Editor: Janet Schwind
Graphic Designer: Suzanne Parada

The views and information expressed in this manual are those of the authors and are derived from their many years of experience from a pastoral perspective using the Value Exchange method. These views are not in any way linked to that of any organization, employer, church, ministry, establishment or individual. The authors are not licensed counselors, psychiatrists or psychologists and make no claims to be giving professional counseling advice or that the materials be used in lieu of professional counseling or medical advice. The information provided in this manual is for educational purposes only and does not substitute for professional advice, nor should it be used for the purpose of diagnosing any disorders, whether they be physical or psychological. All the examples given in this manual are fictional and are a compilation of actual life experiences of people, in general. The authors are not responsible for how any person or organization interprets or uses this information nor do the authors guarantee a specific result or outcome from its application or use.

CONTENTS

FOREWORD

I have been writing and compiling Londa's seminar and workshop manuals for almost two decades and have watched the process grow from a few one-page sheets on inner healing to this fully developed manual.

One thing I must attest to, and that is the faithfulness of God the Father. I say this because inner healing is all about Jesus. It is not a "trial and error" method, but rather an "onward and upward" process by which the Holy Spirit brings wisdom, revelation, power, might, knowledge and the fear (reverential trust) of the Lord, whereby those who diligently seek the presence of God will prosper.

There are certain observations one can clearly make, having this ringside seat to all the action. I can truly say that Londa's journey from her heart's pain to peace has been nothing short of epic. Why do I call it epic? Well, it all began in 2002 with a visit to a chiropractic doctor as we were desperate to get her "fixed up" enough to go to the mall without having to use a wheelchair. Chronic pain and fatigue were her constant companions due to advanced fibromyalgia and a couple of other autoimmune diseases. As a result, we were regularly in the doctor's office to get adjustments. Unbeknownst to Londa, the doctor had more than one "adjustment" in mind as he read off a list of negative beliefs, such as *"worthless, not good enough, and unloved,"* and then asked her if any of these phrases applied to her.

"Absolutely not!" was her reply. He encouraged her to pray about that as he turned her over and started working on her back. She began to weep. Afterwards, she sat up and he asked if the Lord shared anything with her about those feelings. She surprised herself by answering, matter-of-factly, "Satan lied to me, and I believed him!"

What? I sat up and straightened my focus on Londa. "God said Satan lied to me, and I believed him!" At that time, neither of us knew that God still talks to us, even though we had been Christians since childhood. But Londa *knew* what she heard that the rest of us didn't hear.

After Londa's visit, the chiropractor gave her an introductory tape on inner healing, and so began that epic journey from constant pain—both in her emotions and in her physical body—to constant peace in her heart as well as many of the ailments and diseases being healed simultaneously. This process also introduced her to an intimate relationship to the One who was giving her peace.

She was focusing on herself exclusively at first, but it wasn't long before she was working with me and other people who wanted to be set free of negative thinking. Early in Londa's ministry, the Lord gave her a passion to write a manual. After more than 15 years and 12,000 hours of one-on-one meetings with hundreds of people, Londa refined her skills and in early 2014, the Lord began to download understanding of a new inner healing method that became known as the Value Exchange.

Londa met Dr. Rachelle Crowder in a divinely appointed meeting in the summer of 2012 to see if she would like to share her testimony at a church service. Rachelle had been miraculously healed from C-diff, a disease she had for 21 months that almost killed her (note: It's bad when the doctor calls the family in to say good-bye). While at a conference they both happened to be attending, Rachelle watched Londa minister inner healing to one of her friends, who experienced total freedom from the emotional pain caused by childhood trauma. Rachelle was speechless and had to know more.

As they met regularly, Londa began to mentor Rachelle in the Value Exchange, which Rachelle, in turn, began to use on herself and her patients and others who wanted prayer. She was amazed about how quickly and effectively the Value Exchange brought emotional healing. Rachelle also realized that people needed to learn this for themselves, prompting her to launch the Value Exchange class in January 2018. She needed teaching materials and so started to put on paper what she learned from Londa. As she reviewed these writings with Londa, she realized there were more "drawers of information" to be pulled out! After thousands of hours of ministry, Londa had presumed, "If I know this, then everyone already knows it too." Rachelle had the privilege of being trained by Londa—watching her do sessions with other people, having sessions with Londa for her own healing, and just spending lots of time with her. In this process, Londa and Rachelle's friendship matured and they became best friends. Eventually they spent their free day together each week to intentionally write this manual. For both of them, it's been a "labor" of love.

The Value Exchange is a comprehensive, practical manual to overcoming all the common negative feelings and beliefs we experience as imperfect humans, and the coping mechanisms we attach to them. *The Value Exchange* is also a supernatural encounter that brings the heart and mind together to be in right alignment with God's truth. It is an invaluable reference, ready to assist in any circumstance of the heart. I am witness to this epic journey and I say epic because of this:

> Merriam-Webster defines epic (adjective) as:
>
> a: extending beyond the usual or ordinary especially
>   in size or scope
> b: HEROIC

This friendship was borne out of the common desire for union with the Father, Son, and Holy Spirit, and the Value Exchange has been the primary vehicle for removing "every obstacle and the sin which so easily entangles us" [Heb 12:1 NASB] and receiving peace with the Father through Jesus Christ.

I stand as a witness to both Londa and Rachelle in that they have been diligent where many have grown weary, and they continue to pursue intimacy with God with amazing results. So, I am honored to write this foreword to a work that has been, indeed, a labor of love to all people who want free from the lies and deception that keep us from the relationship we *all* are created to have with the Almighty and with each other.

Christopher Harwell
January 2022

INTRODUCTION

The Value Exchange is an opportunity to give Jesus your painful feelings and beliefs in exchange for His supernatural perspective. You will be giving Him your painful feelings, along with the coping mechanisms you've attached to them. In return, you will receive healing and your mind and heart will come into unity and peace. This is not another coping mechanism. This is not a "Band-Aid" approach. This is literally getting complete freedom from your past hurts.

Most of us grow up with the understanding that conversation with God is one-sided. We pray. He listens. We are told we need to pray to God but find ourselves talking *to* Him, not really knowing *how* to hear from Him. Because He is invisible, having a conversation with God is not going to be like talking to the person sitting next to you. Using our method of heart-and-mind healing called the Value Exchange, you will learn how to receive from the Lord those things that are on His heart for you, resulting in a true heart-to-heart connection. This will open up a whole new relationship of intimacy between you and God.

Isn't it amazing that you can personally communicate with the one true God who created you?! You have the privilege to know *the* one and only, unique and holy God because of what Jesus did for you on the cross! You were separated from God because of your sins and unholiness. God is the source of life and separation from Him brings death. Jesus took your punishment, giving Him the legal right to bring you into right relationship with God (Colossians 1:12-14). After rising from the dead, Jesus returned to Heaven and then gave the gift of the Holy Spirit to anyone who repents of sin and invites Jesus to be Lord and Savior of their heart. The Holy Spirit then joins with your spirit and you are reborn into the Kingdom of God—a child of God (Romans 8:16)!

The Holy Spirit connects you with God, Jesus, and the invisible spirit realm. In a way, Holy Spirit acts like an "antenna" of communication. Jesus talks about Holy Spirit in John 14:26 (AMP), stating, "But the Helper (Comforter, Advocate, Intercessor, Counselor, Strengthener, Standby), the Holy Spirit, whom the Father will send in My name (in My place, to represent me and act on My behalf), He will teach you all things. And He will help you remember everything that I have told you." You will need to know how to communicate with Holy Spirit to receive His help, comfort, counsel and strength.

In the last decade, the New Age Movement has become a popular way to connect with the spirit realm using spirit guides. With the Value Exchange method, you will be connecting only with the Holy Spirit. In Greek, the word holy means "pure, morally blameless" and "set apart." His holiness is difficult to describe or understand because it is so completely opposite of anything we have ever seen or experienced in our world. In fact, God is so holy that no one can look at Him and live (Exodus 33:20)! In light of this truth, we can understand why we need the Holy Spirit to enable us to communicate with God.

Jesus was willing to pour out His life to death, offering Himself as a guilt offering for YOU (Isaiah 53:10,12). He was wounded, crushed and punished instead of YOU (Isaiah 53:4,5). The punishment for YOUR well-being fell on Him (Isaiah 53:5). He paid a high price for you and then gives you the Holy Spirit as a gift. Holy Spirit's desire is to develop a love relationship with you.

HOLY SPIRIT'S DESIRE IS TO DEVELOP A LOVE RELATIONSHIP WITH YOU.

As you prepare to hear from the Lord, recognize that Holy Spirit has many ways to interact with you. You might suddenly get a picture in your mind, remember a time from the past, or have a thought (including a song, poem, scripture, etc.) just pop into your head. If I asked you to picture an elephant, you would do that pretty quickly and effortlessly. Holy Spirit can put things into your mind quickly too! You just have to be open to hearing and then be aware of your thoughts. If you get a picture or phrase but don't understand what it means, ask Holy Spirit to give you understanding. Be sure to position your heart by clearing your mind of everything you think the picture or phrase could mean. You don't need to figure it out. Just be open to receiving. He will give you understanding. If understanding doesn't come to you, it's possible that the picture is not from the Lord. At this point, state, "If this is not from the true Lord Jesus, then I command it to go! Lord Jesus, what do You want me to know?"

Sometimes you might not think about anything but have a feeling of peace. That is Him speaking too! His voice has a quality about it that feels very peaceful. He will never speak harshly, mock, or make you feel bad. He is very loving, kind, and unbelievably patient. In His holiness, it is impossible for Him to lie, and He will always speak truth. The truth He speaks will resonate with your heart, and you'll be able to receive it and the healing His voice brings. His voice has absolute authority, and your spirit will respond to it. It's possible to speak truth to yourself and not receive healing. But when God speaks that same truth to you, your heart will receive it.

You might experience physical symptoms as you receive from Him. You might yawn or feel like stretching. Your body may suddenly relax. You may feel tingling or goose bumps! The world might appear brighter, you may notice a sound you hadn't heard before, smell something new, or see something in the room you hadn't previously noticed. If so, you could ask the Lord what He wants you to know about what He just showed you. It's even possible for you to receive physical healing in the exchange.

Thoughts come from three sources: your own mind (conscious or subconscious), God, or the demonic. The enemy inserts thoughts into our mind and we don't even know it. For example, if you got publicly reprimanded at work for making a mistake, you might hear yourself thinking, "I'm a failure" or "I'm stupid." Because you made a mistake, the mistake becomes evidence that these beliefs are true. The enemy will continue to remind you of this "truth," desiring to create a negative stronghold in your thought life. The more we agree with him, the louder his voice becomes. We really need to become aware of whose voice we are listening to.

The way to recognize the enemy's voice is to know what the voice of God is like. God's voice will always line up with God's character. The enemy's voice may sound directly condemning or negative in some way, making you feel worse. However, his voice may not always line up with his own evil character. His power is deception, and he wields it expertly, leading you down a pathway of half-truths, like a "truth with a twist" on it. For instance, you may hear the message, "You are forgiven, but you need to read the Bible more, memorize scripture, and spend time in worship. Then you will *feel* forgiven." All those things are good, but the word "but" makes it sound like feeling forgiven is dependent on you working harder; this does not line up with what the scripture says. When we sincerely ask for forgiveness, we *are forgiven*. It's a gift and we don't have to work to receive it.

When the Lord speaks, it will always line up with the scripture and His character. The enemy wants you to believe that what he says is coming from God. For example, he may say, "It's okay to be angry with that person. It's understandable." He's telling you what you want to hear, justifying unforgiveness. This is the exact opposite of what God says about unforgiveness in scripture (Mark 11:25-26).

As you confront the negative feelings and beliefs during a Value Exchange encounter, it's possible you might feel negative physical symptoms. For instance, you could experience sudden nausea, a headache, ear ringing, throat tightening, pressure or squeezing in your chest or other physical symptoms. These things are uncomfortable and may feel scary. In truth, they are indications that you're very close to having freedom! Don't be intimidated by them, because once your Value Exchange is finished, all those symptoms will go away!

As you read this manual, you'll be given the opportunity to engage the Lord in prayer to receive His truths, perspective, and help. You'll be asked to take time at the end of each prayer to receive from the Lord. Remember to do that! Enjoy this time together, as the Author and Creator of Life, the Lover of your Soul, fills you with His love and truth. He will feed your soul with revelations from His heart, giving you new identity, purpose, and destiny.

CHAPTER 1

THE VALUE EXCHANGE
What is it?

The Value Exchange is a tool that enables you to recognize, confront, and release painful emotions along with their negative beliefs. It will also teach you how to receive from the Lord because *He is the one* who will personally communicate with you. He will find a way to communicate with your heart, whether it is by hearing, a picture, sudden understanding, or some other means unique to you and Him. He knows what you need and how to communicate in a way you can receive. You'll gain understanding of the many ways the enemy has deceived you into believing lies about yourself or God. These lies *feel true* in the moment, causing you to act and react out of negative emotion rather than wisdom and peace. Whether you realize it or not, *you really do have a choice* whether to accept these emotions or beliefs as truth. These negative emotions and beliefs are empowered because you have, on some level, believed them to be true and do not know how to make them go away.

Our well-being is determined by what we believe.
Therefore, what we believe is extremely important.

Everyone has been wounded by people or situations and needs healing. Whether it is intentional or not, our mind will try to figure out how to think about what just happened that wounded us. Unfortunately, most of us carry the impact of our wounds for years, decades, and sometimes throughout our entire lives because we just cannot shake how those traumatic moments made us feel. We struggle with feeling inferior or stressed, e.g., trying to give those feelings or beliefs to Jesus—only to discover we took them back again! We can't even remember how or why we took them back! Using the Value Exchange as a tool, you will be learning how to receive lasting healing as your thinking aligns with the mind of Christ rather than with your unrenewed mind.

> **Therefore I urge you, brethren, by the mercies of God, to present your bodies a living and holy sacrifice, acceptable to God, which is your spiritual service of worship. And do not be conformed to this world, but *be transformed by the renewing of your mind*, so that you may prove what the will of God is, that which is good, and acceptable and perfect.**
> *~Romans 12:1-2* (NASB)

First, we must understand what happens in the *moment* of trauma or pain.

At the *very moment* of wounding, emotional pain rises up within us. Our mind will instantly try to react by figuring out how to process what just happened to us. By thinking, we *sort it out* and then determine what to believe about what just happened. The emotion seems to have a voice of its own, speaking a message into our heart about ourselves that feels true in the moment. This wounding is the perfect opportunity for the demonic to insert their opinions/lies about you.

For example, you may have experienced a teacher reprimanding you in front of the class for not studying enough, resulting in a bad grade on your test. You initially feel shamed and humiliated, wondering what the other kids will think about you now. Your mind starts to sort out what just happened and how to think about it. Then a belief starts to form. The teacher made you feel stupid and like a failure in front of everyone! The belief you conclude is, "I'm stupid" and then, "I'm a failure." Note the progression of negative thoughts. In this way, the enemy plants lie-based seeds into your heart and you choose whether to believe these messages or not. The more often you make mistakes, the more you hear and believe those same lies. You allow them to fester and they become more empowered. At some point, the lies you believe feel true, describing how you really see yourself.

What you believe about yourself will play out in your life in some way. You'll live from that perceived reality, allowing it to determine how you act and react. This belief can become a stronghold in your mind, acting like a control station from which you make all future decisions.

According to physicists, negative thoughts and emotions contain negative energy or waves. In fact, you can feel a person's negative or positive atmosphere sometimes when you enter a room. This negative energy arises out of a wound and a stronghold begins to form. These strongholds create the way you will think and feel about everything concerning your life. They give you a *new lens,* or perspective, of seeing the world. Living from the lens of the labels "I'm stupid" and "I'm a failure" looks a lot different than living from the lens of feeling "I'm smart" and "I'm capable." The failure/stupid lens would cause you to fear doing new things by taking away your confidence. The lens of smart/capable would cause you to feel confident about trying new things.

> The Value Exchange will expose the reasons why these negative strongholds are so hard to overcome. Then you'll be able to come before the Lord in an encounter where you can give up the lie-based stronghold in exchange for His Truth.

As time passes, you might find yourself repeatedly being triggered by situations not even remotely related to the original event that caused you to believe "I'm stupid and I'm a failure." As the years go by, you may find yourself struggling internally to believe in yourself even though you have some level of success and accomplishments under your belt. These reactions happen without you intentionally being aware of them because they're planted deeply in the subconscious parts of your mind. Once they are in place, they feel impossible to remove!

Have you ever felt like the apostle Paul when he said, "What a miserable creature I am!" in Romans 7:24 (CJB)? How do we find victory when we have taken on strongholds like anxiety, fear, doubt, feeling not good enough, or stupid? When feelings or beliefs like these become strongholds, we are not under the protective stronghold of the Lord. His protection would keep us in a place of feeling loved and valued regardless of how other people treat us. **The Value Exchange will expose the reasons why these negative strongholds are so hard to overcome. Then you'll be able to come before the Lord in an encounter where you can give up the lie-based stronghold in exchange for His Truth.** We then can live in the Truth of what *He says* rather than from the lies we believed.

To overcome strongholds, we need to know more about how they're created. They typically begin the moment you feel emotional or physical pain. These bad experiences often happen unexpectedly, which makes it very difficult to know how to respond. This unpleasant emotion you are feeling in the moment will cause you to respond in some manner. You will subconsciously try to find a way to avoid pain again. In the moment of wounding, the emotional pain and lie feel true. Then based on that truth, you reach for something to help you deal with this new reality. By developing coping mechanisms, you hope to avoid feeling emotional pain again.

The illustration on the next page starts with the moment of wounding (the painful emotion leading to the lie/belief), which then causes you to search for a way to cope. The coping mechanism you reach for is inspired by negative emotions/beliefs. By using the coping mechanism, it becomes attached to wounded thinking. In this way, coping mechanisms are birthed from wounded thinking. The feeling has become an alert to use the attached coping mechanisms. If the wound has been present long enough, you can attach a lot of coping mechanisms!

Wounded thinking (feelings/beliefs), along with attached coping mechanisms, create a "package deal." To get healing you will need to give up the coping mechanism(s) attached to the wound.

WOUNDED THINKING + COPING MECHANISMS = PACKAGE DEAL

(how that makes me feel/what I believe)

WOUND
emotion/belief

+

COPING MECHANISMS

= PACKAGE DEAL

YOU WILL NEED TO GIVE UP
THE ENTIRE PACKAGE
DEAL **TO BE HEALED!**

The enemy deceives you into believing you need this coping mechanism "package" to survive and navigate life. You might not have any concept of what life would be without it. Giving it away would feel like a bad mistake! You use this package to protect your heart, but by doing so, you are DISPLACING the Holy Spirit, whose desire is to protect you. This demonically inspired package wants to tell you how to think. If you allow this package to remain and influence your thinking, it will result in your mind being taken captive.

For example, if I'm in a meeting and start to feel like I'm stupid and a failure, then I react by not participating in the discussion to protect myself from looking bad. The shame of believing "I'm stupid and a failure" alerts me to the threat of looking bad and I now protect myself by not participating in the discussion. These negative beliefs will further motivate me to avoid people and situations that might trigger that same feeling. However, the perceived protection of avoiding people and situations is really keeping me from healthy interactions, setting and achieving goals, and living life to the fullest. This coping mechanism of self-protection affects relationships with family, friends, and colleagues. Alternatively, this belief may become a motivator, causing me to work harder to avoid looking bad.

WOUNDED THINKING + COPING MECHANISMS = PACKAGE DEAL

Shame makes me think:	Shame makes me do:	Wounded thinking/Coping Mechanism = Package Deal
I'm stupid	Self-motivates to work harder	I'm stupid - motivation
I'm a failure	Self-protection by avoidance	I'm a failure - protection

In another example, let's say that as a child you were sexually molested and verbally abused by your sibling's friend on multiple occasions. In those moments of trauma, you felt shame and then believed you were ugly and dirty. The shame also made you feel like "damaged goods" and "nobody could love me if they knew what happened." Those feelings and beliefs will cause you to find a way to cope with them. Your response may be to put up an emotional wall to keep people pushed away, not allowing them to get close to your heart or be able to hurt you. You may believe "I'm only good for sex," which may give you an excuse to become promiscuous, hoping to earn love or get attention.

WOUNDED THINKING + COPING MECHANISMS = PACKAGE DEAL

Shame makes me think:	Shame makes me do:	Wounded thinking/Coping Mechanism = Package Deal
I'm ugly and dirty	Put up an emotional wall of protection	I'm ugly and dirty - wall
I'm damaged goods	Avoid intimate relationships so nobody finds out	I'm damaged goods - avoidance
Nobody could love me if they found out	Sabotage a relationship that is getting too serious	Nobody could love me - protection
I'm only good for sex	Act promiscuous to earn love or get attention	I'm only good for sex - to earn love and get attention

We want to get rid of our wounded thinking and emotional pain, but we may not be willing to give up the value of the coping mechanisms attached to it.

The perceived VALUE that the coping mechanism has for us keeps our wounded thinking in place.

Until you give up your coping mechanisms, you will not be free from the pain. You are also giving *the very people who hurt you* the power to determine your self-worth, which will negatively affect your well-being!

Your first step in the healing process will be to identify the following:

1) What you're feeling and believing

2) What coping mechanism you're using

Here's where the Value Exchange comes in. Armed with the awareness of your wounded thinking and coping mechanisms, you will give Jesus permission to remove the value of this "package deal" and give you what He has for you in exchange. In doing this, you'll exchange the pain and lies for healing and the truth of Jesus.

REMEMBER, YOU'LL NEED TO GIVE UP THE ENTIRE PACKAGE DEAL TO BE HEALED!

You need to embrace mind renewal if you're going to move forward in life and become all that God has created you to be. The Bible tells us to be active in the transformation of our minds. With this tool, you will see your mind and life transformed!

> **So prepare your minds for action, be completely sober**
> **(in spirit—steadfast, self-disciplined, spiritually and morally**
> **alert), fix your hope completely on the grace (of God) that**
> **is coming to you when Jesus Christ is revealed.**
> *~1 Peter 1:13* *(AMP)*

Mind transformation occurs when we *choose* to allow the Lord to humble us and give **His perspective** of our misdirected thinking. Keeping and using negative emotions, beliefs, and their coping mechanisms instead of relying on the Lord means we are operating out of a lack of faith. We're finding shelter in our false structures instead of the Lord.

When those negative emotions and beliefs are present, they become the distorted lens through which we see life. This lens gives us a perspective that contradicts the Truth that God sees in us as His child. Mind renewal requires active participation and the *"want to"* engage the Holy Spirit for His truth, perspective, and healing. Holy Spirit will not enter where He is not invited. As we allow the Lord to heal our minds by exchanging the lie(s) we believe for His truth, our perspective is brought into unity and harmony with Him. We will then begin to think, act, and react like Jesus! In this act of mind renewal, we partake of His divine nature and share in His glory! Oh, what an amazing interaction between us and our Jesus!

> **But we all, with unveiled face, beholding as in a mirror the**
> **glory of the Lord, are being *transformed* into the same image**
> **from glory to glory, just as from the Lord, the Spirit.**
> *~2 Corinthians 3:18* *(NASB)*

God has a countermeasure for every scheme the enemy has used to wound us. The Lord wants to be *the Voice* of Truth to us. He is aware of every hurtful event and abuse (physical, emotional, and spiritual) we have suffered. By the power and help of the Holy Spirit, these hurts can be exposed and released to Him in EXCHANGE for His healing and truth. The Value Exchange is a method of praying in such a way that you will encounter the Lord and be able to receive the healing He paid for YOU to have. When you have the *"want to,"* the Value Exchange will give you the *"how to."*

By following these steps, you'll successfully take yourself through the process of renewing your mind. Jesus will *always* give you something of Kingdom value in exchange for what you're giving up. It is important that you do not analyze or explain away the pain. Logic will **not** bring about true healing of wounded emotions. Healed emotions will result in right thinking and bring you into alignment and unity with Christ.

STEPS TO FREEDOM

1. Identify your wounded thinking: The negative emotion, feelings and/or belief (stronghold).

What would you like Jesus to help you with? What emotion have you been wrestling with or trying not to feel? What do you believe about yourself that you cannot shake? Are you struggling with feeling "not good enough," anxiety or fear? Are you having trouble forgiving someone? Do you struggle to believe God loves you and cares about your well-being? Are you angry with God?

Allow yourself to observe your thoughts and become aware of what your subconscious mind is believing. You might have to give yourself permission to do this because allowing yourself to admit you truly have these unhealthy thoughts may be hard. We know we are not supposed to feel or think this way. But you need to know what your mind and heart are really feeling. This tool will help you get in touch with what's going on in the subconscious part of your mind. In the first part of the equation, you will identify what kind of emotion you're feeling (like shame, fear, sadness, etc.). Then identify the belief attached to it (for example, "shame makes me feel like I'm worthless").

It's important to know that analyzing a memory will take you down the wrong pathway and HINDER your progress. You only need to recognize what YOU feel or believe. Everything else goes on a shelf. Do not try to figure out the "why" questions.

> **Trust and rely confidently on the lord with all your heart**
> **and do not rely on your own insight or understanding.**
> **In all your ways know and acknowledge and recognize**
> **Him, and He will make your paths straight and smooth**
> **(removing obstacles that block your way).**
> *~Proverbs 3:5-6* *(AMP)*

2. Identify each coping mechanism and its value.

The negative feeling and belief will cause you to react in a way to protect yourself and help you avoid feeling uncomfortable again. Ask yourself how you might be using this negative feeling and its accompanying belief to navigate life to avoid pain. These negative feelings and emotions will cause you to do things to self-protect, self-motivate, self-elevate/promote, self-comfort, or take justice into your hands. It is possible to have other uses unique to you.

The following are some examples of common coping mechanisms and their values/benefits to you.

a. Self-protection:

1. Fear could cause me to stay on guard, ready for the next bad thing to happen. By doing this, I am trusting fear to protect me.

2. Feelings of failure may cause me to avoid taking chances.

3. Feeling God doesn't care about me and isn't involved in my life could cause me to stop expecting Him to care or be involved. Doing this would keep my heart from feeling hurt when He doesn't show up or intervene in the future the way I think He should.

4. Feelings of "not good enough" may cause me to keep a "wall up" around friends to protect my heart from being hurt.

b. Self-motivation:

1. Feeling "not good enough" may cause me to try harder to be better.

2. Feeling out of control may cause me to become controlling so I feel safe.

c. Self-elevation/promotion:

1. Feeling like a failure may cause me to do things that make me look better so I can measure up to other people. It can also motivate me to "show off" to feel better than other people.

2. Feeling "not good enough" may cause me to take on perfectionism, which is an attempt to make me look really good in the eyes of people. In this way, people will "look up" to me.

3. Feeling worthless may cause me to take on an addiction to pornography so I can feel valuable in my fantasies.

   Self-elevation is always pride-based, inflating the perception of how you see yourself and how you want others to see you. In this way, you bring glory and attention to yourself.

d. Self-comfort:

1. Feeling unloved may cause me to comfort myself with pity. It feels good to feel sorry for myself. "I'm the only one to have this happen. You don't know what I've been through. You're not living it. Others may want to join me!"

2. Feeling worthless may cause me to take on an addiction to _____ _____ for comfort.

3. When I feel out of control and pressured, or feel bad about myself, I can find comfort by watching pornography; fantasizing brings a physical and emotional release.

4. Intense feelings of being rejected, unloved, shamed, etc., can cause me to cut (or otherwise hurt) myself to release the pain of those beliefs and bring comfort.

5. Feeling out of control in many areas of my life can cause me to reach for food for comfort because it's something "I can control" and is socially acceptable.

e. Self-justice:

1. Feeling disrespected may cause me to get revenge or use anger to take justice. I might fantasize about being the judge or "righting" the wrong myself.

2. The emotional pain from being abused as a child may cause me to withhold forgiving my abuser as a way to take justice, because it keeps them punished. The unforgiveness feels like I am bringing justice.

3. Get an *understanding* of the value of the coping mechanism you have attached to the wounded emotion or belief.

Take a moment to look closer. Can you see the value you've assigned to each coping mechanism you've employed? How has it helped you avoid pain and discomfort? Can you recognize the value of the coping mechanism you'll need to give up? If you need help understanding, ask the Holy Spirit,

"Could You help me understand the value I've given to the coping mechanism(s) attached to this emotion/belief? Can You show me what this coping mechanism looks like in the spirit?" (This will look good to you because you are using it as a benefit.)

4. Assess your willingness to give up the value.

Ask yourself, *"Do I have any objections or resistance to giving up the value of this?"*

You may want to picture Jesus in front of you, place the value before Him, and ask yourself if you're willing to let Him take it. For example, you may value the comfort and control of overeating when you're feeling emotional pain. How would you feel about handing the comfort and control over to Jesus? Do you feel any resistance to letting it go?

If there is no resistance to giving up the value, then proceed to the next step.

If there is resistance, then proceed to the section on Dealing With Resistance later in this chapter.

Jesus will not take the value if you are not willing to giving it up.

5. Picture yourself before Jesus and place the value of the coping mechanism before Him on the altar (or hand it to Him) and then say the Value Exchange prayer.

By picturing Jesus, you're giving Him permission to speak to you, and it may help you engage Him more easily. The altar is a place where you're making a sacrifice by giving up something of value you have used to cope with the pain. If possible, say these prayers out loud.

Value Exchange Prayer:

Jesus, I recognize I have been holding onto the feeling of:

_____

_____

and/or the belief of _____

_____

I have attached the coping mechanism of:

_____

_____

in order to _____

_____

(protect myself, motivate myself, elevate/promote myself, take justice, comfort myself (or other).

I ask Your forgiveness for doing this.

I now choose to break agreement with this emotion/belief (stronghold)

of: _____

_____

and I give up all the value of _____

_____ *I have placed on it.*

I command all demonic (ungodly) assignments that have come against me because of this to go now, in Jesus' name!

6. Ask the Lord to remove the wounded emotion/belief and its connected coping mechanism/value and give you what He has in exchange.

Jesus, I ask You to clean this place out for me and give me what You have in exchange.

After saying this prayer, PAUSE and take time to receive from the Lord. This is not something you'll need to make happen. There is no pressure. Don't try to figure out what He might say or do. Just sit back and receive. Your heart WILL be able to receive from Him and you'll be able to agree with His truth.

**"The sheep that are My own hear My voice and listen to Me;
I know them, and they follow Me."**
~John 10:27 (AMP)

7. Check to see how you feel now.

After receiving the Value Exchange, check to see if the negative feeling/belief is still there. Can you still feel that emotion? Does that belief still feel true?

If not, then go to Step 8.

If you still feel the emotion and the belief still feels true, then there may be an unaddressed coping mechanism/value connected to it and you need to return to Step 2. It's also possible that you have some resistance to giving this up. If so, then go to the end of this chapter on Dealing with Resistance.

8. Test the healing in a memory.

Always, always, always go back into a memory you know previously contained the wounded emotion/belief to see if it is still there. Sometimes you have memories that are hard to go back into because they contain a lot of trauma. Ask Jesus to go into that memory with you to look at the *one* emotional part you just worked on. Would you give yourself permission to check for only that one emotion?

Check the memory even if you're not sure what you received in the exchange. You'll be able to see things from a new perspective (His!) and the negative emotion/belief should be gone. There should be peace. If there's still pain in the memory, then you need to identify the remaining feeling and belief. Sometimes there are *layers* of feelings and beliefs in a memory and these new areas will be exposed. Don't be discouraged. Take one negative emotion at a time. You have an opportunity to get more healing. Eventually this memory will become peaceful, no matter how packed it was. Go back to #1 and prepare for another exchange!

Again, return to the memory with Jesus and check to see how you're feeling now about the person/people who hurt you. Do you feel like you can forgive them? Do you have compassion for them? The feeling of compassion shows you have reached a very deep level of healing and forgiveness. If you still feel unforgiveness toward them, ask yourself why you're not willing to forgive and then go back to #1 and do another exchange until the memory is clear. You're making progress with each Value Exchange!

9. Undealt-with negative emotions may have an impact on your physical body. Even though the emotion has been removed from your mind and heart by the Value Exchange, the body may still hold the memory of that old wound. This can be released from your body by saying the following prayer:

I recognize that this emotional pain has impacted my health. I choose to break agreement with all the negative health consequences affecting my body. I command all demonic assignments directed toward my body to go, in Jesus' name! Lord Jesus, I ask You to clean this out of my body and bring Your healing touch to every part affected by woundedness.

Be sure to take time to receive from the Lord.

If you have been experiencing physical disease or pain, this is a good time to check for healing. For instance, if you have chronic back pain, then try doing an activity that would usually cause pain. Remember to keep blessing your body.

A free wallet-sized card for you to print and laminate is available on our website, **FreedomExpress16.org**. With this, you can keep the Value Exchange prayer readily available and pull it out whenever you need it.

DEALING WITH RESISTANCE

Sometimes it can be hard to give up the value of our coping mechanisms. If you had resistance in question #4, there are several ways to overcome it.

Set the emotion/belief and its attached coping mechanism/value before the Lord and ask Him questions about them.

Engaging the Lord in conversation is always the wisest thing to do when you need help. When you choose to involve Him in this way, you don't have to worry that He will take the coping mechanism/value away from you. He's happy to help you evaluate it and see it from His perspective. Even though the coping mechanism seems like a good thing, it was birthed from a negative emotion and belief. Because this comes from a negative energy source (the kingdom of darkness), the coping mechanism will come with a negative consequence, which isn't always obvious at first. The enemy tricks us into using these coping mechanisms by disguising them as something that's helpful. Even though they feel helpful initially, they have a hidden, evil agenda that will eventually cause problems, bringing fear, lack and/or distress into your life.

REMEMBER, DEMONS ARE CLEVER AND PROFESSIONALS AT DECEPTION. DO YOU WANT TO KNOW THE TRUTH?

In contrast, positive energy from the Kingdom of God brings peace, love, and joy, which are the fruits of righteousness (right standing with God). Jesus will always give you something better than what you will give up in this exchange. You don't want to fight a negative emotion/belief with a negative solution. Remind yourself—you are resisting giving something up that is demonically inspired and nothing good can come from it.

In some cases, you may even recognize you have come into agreement with an actual demon to provide protection or benefit you in some way. At some level, you're not seeing the truth about this negative emotion/belief and its way of coping. Remember, demons are clever and professionals at deception. Do you want to know the truth?

For example, fear is the expectation of something bad happening. If I hold onto fear, I can use it as self-protection. In this way, when something bad DOES happen, you feel "padded from the blow" because you were on guard and ready. Fear also might keep you from doing things that feel risky. Giving up fear's protection would make you feel vulnerable and unprotected. The enemy seriously messes with your mind to trick you into trusting in fear for your protection. Wouldn't you think FEAR would be a very scary protector?! You could picture yourself handing the package consisting of fear (and its attached value of protection) to Jesus, or even putting it on a table while you both look at it together. Remember, He is completely trustworthy and will always tell you the truth about it. You can talk to Him as a trusted best friend. You're asking for His opinion. Some examples of questions to ask Jesus are the following:

1. *"Jesus, what are Your thoughts about how I've used this coping mechanism of _____ to help me?"*

2. *"Jesus, could You share Your heart with me about the belief that I **need** _____ (e.g., fear) to protect myself, motivate myself, elevate myself, comfort myself, or take justice?"*

3. *"Jesus, what does the value of this coping mechanism look like to You?"*

4. *"Jesus, could You show me how I'm being deceived by exposing the true demonic intent of the coping mechanism?"*

Sometimes you just can't imagine life without the coping mechanism because it's all you've ever known. In this case, you might want to ask Jesus to show you what life would be like if He took it and gave you the exchange. Recognize that in doing this, He won't take it away from you. He *will* give you a new way to think, or He *will* let you keep it if that's what you choose. For example, you might ask,

"Jesus, I've been using this belief/emotion/coping mechanism to protect myself for so long that I can't imagine life without it. But I give you permission to show me what my life would be like if I gave it up and allowed You to give me something else in exchange."

If you're feeling really intense emotional pain or fear, it may be impossible to hear or receive anything from the Lord. Even though the enemy may have such strong control of your mind right now, you still have power over him and need to use your authority to push those emotions back so you can think.

> *"I take authority over the power of this emotion/belief and command it to back off, in Jesus' name!"*

After doing this, you should get some emotional space to be able to have a conversation with Jesus. Then go back to the questions listed above.

After you've broken through the resistance, then go back to Step 5 to complete a Value Exchange.

HOLDING ONTO YOUR HEALING

CONGRATULATIONS! You've received healing from the Lord through a Value Exchange! That's a celebration! Jesus, through Holy Spirit, has come to you and healed you in a very tangible and real way! As you continue to go to Him with all your negative feelings and beliefs, you will continue to experience healing and deepen in your relationship with Him.

Even though the enemy of our souls has lost ground, the war for our minds never ends. You'll need to learn to stand in the healing you have received. The enemy is not happy about losing ground and will continue attempts to poke or trigger you, trying to get you to take back those wrong beliefs and emotions, along with their coping mechanisms. *Remember—the trigger is only a temptation to take it back.* Often, the trigger is so hard it already feels like you've taken it back. When this happens, you must stand your ground. You could picture that emotion or wrong belief speaking into your ear, tempting you to believe it. You need to speak out loud and command it to GO, in Jesus' name, and then ask Him to tell you what He wants you to KNOW in exchange. It's like pushing the negative out of the way so you can hear His voice. You may want to speak the following:

> *"I command (feeling/belief) to **GO**, in Jesus' name!*
> *Lord Jesus, what do You want me to **KNOW** in exchange?"*

To "know" means to perceive directly and to have understanding of. You're receiving a Kingdom, rather than a fleshy, worldly perspective. Receive the truth of what He has for you. MOVE THAT BAD EMOTION OR BELIEF OUT OF THE WAY!!! Tell it to take a hike! Sometimes with all the busyness of life we forget to take time to stop what we're doing and listen for His voice. Will you pause and invite Him into the moments of your life? He is your very special friend who has made Himself available to you at any time! His home is within you. He stands at the doorway of your heart waiting. It's unfortunate that the busyness of the day can keep us from doing something so simple. We should seek His opinion and wisdom all the time!

> **So stand firm and hold your ground, having tightened the wide band of truth (personal integrity, moral courage) around your waist and having put on the breastplate of righteousness (an upright heart) …**
> ~ *Ephesians 6:14* (AMP)

Prayer:

My heart aches with love for You, Lord. The more I learn to love You, the more I want to love. I invite You, Father, to strip me of all distractions until You alone are all I see. I want to sit and gaze on Your beauty, to behold You in all Your glory. Your splendor leaves me without words sufficient to describe what I see. I am filled with awe for You, Lord, and I want more. I want to sit at Your feet and learn from You the mysteries of Your heart. I want to know what You are seeing, feeling and saying. Your truths are simple yet profound. Teach me to be a good listener, Lord. I want to know You as the Lover of my heart, to experience Your love deep within my heart, so that my heart looks like Yours—love so pure and holy, so undefiled. One thing I know about You, Lord, is that love originates from You! Because that is who You are. Every motive in Your heart comes from perfect, unconditional love. Thank You, Lord, that I can trust Your love.

CHAPTER 2

Finding the Value/Coping Mechanisms

B elow are examples of how you could be using negative feelings and/ or beliefs, then turning them into something that *feels* positive and therefore has value. This is not always easy to understand or figure out. Remember to look at what you're doing in response to the pain or belief.

1. If I hold onto _____ (anxiety/fear, etc.), then I won't be caught off guard and will be ready for it.

2. If I hold onto _____ (anxiety/fear, etc.), then I won't feel vulnerable.

3. If I hold onto _____ (disappointment/ hopelessness, etc.), then I won't be as disappointed.

4. If I hold onto _____ (failure, not good enough, worthless, rejected, etc.), then I won't risk being rejected, left out or overlooked.

5. If I hold onto _____ (anxiety/fear, etc.), then I can feel more in control and safe.

6. If I hold onto _____ (anger, unforgiveness, etc.), then I'll feel more powerful instead of being controlled or dominated.

7. I can use _____ anger/unforgiveness/ resentment/bitterness/hatred, etc.) to bring justice where there was injustice.

8. I can use _____ (anger/unforgiveness, etc.) to punish them and prevent the people who hurt me from getting too close again.

9. I can use _____ (anxiety, not good enough, failure, depression, shame, etc.) to motivate me to try harder to be better.

10. If I hold onto _____ (failure, shame, not good enough, etc.), then I don't have to do things and risk making a mistake or getting into trouble.

11. _____ (worry, anxiety, etc.) makes me feel like I'm doing something about the problem or helps me figure it out.

12. _____ (depression, failure, etc.) keeps me from having to do something I don't want to do.

13. _____ (anger, pride, being controlling, etc.) gives me power so I don't feel powerless.

14. _____ (fear, anxiety, powerless, etc.) feels comfortable because I've never known life without it. To give it up would be scary.

15. _____ (worthless, unforgiveness, etc.) puts up a protective boundary/wall to keep them from getting too close.

16. _____ (people pleasing, promiscuity, etc.) brings me attention so I feel loved.

17. If I hold onto _____ (inferiority, worthless, etc.), then I know my place and that feels safe.

18. If I hold onto _____ (helplessness, not good enough, inferiority, etc.), it will help keep me humble.

19. If I hold onto _____ (rejection, unloved, etc.), then I'm protected from the pain of rejection.

20. It's better to expect _____ (rejection, anger, etc.) than to be caught off guard! I'll know what to expect.

21. If I hold onto _____ (guilt, self-condemnation, etc.), then it will keep me from making a mistake like that again.

22. If I hold onto _____ (unforgiveness, anger, etc.), it feels like I'm protecting myself from them hurting me again like that.

23. If I hold onto _____ (anxiety, stress, etc.), then I'll be motivated to take action.

24. If I hold onto _____ (unforgiveness, anger, etc.), then it will convict them that what they did was wrong.

25. If I hold onto _____ (unforgiveness, anger, etc.), for example, holding onto pain to prove I'm right, what they did was wrong and they don't deserve forgiveness), then it will justify why I can't forgive them.

26. If I hold onto _____ (disappointment, rejection, etc.), then I won't expect as much or be hurt as badly.

27. If I hold onto _____ (confusion, etc.), it will protect me from making a mistake or the wrong decision.

28. If I let this_____ (pornography, addictions, masturbation, etc.) go, then I won't have a way to comfort myself.

29. I could hold onto _____ (self-pity, depression, etc.) because people feel sorry for me and I get more attention.

30. I could hold onto _____ (self-pity, etc.) because it feels good to feel sad.

CHAPTER 3

God Issues

God issues are feelings and beliefs about God *that don't line up with what the Bible says about God*. Usually, these beliefs or feelings are a result of misunderstanding hurtful events that happened in our life. These perceptions will cause us to question God's character.

Children will naturally look at their parents—especially their father—as a representation of what God is like. In doing this, we are bringing God down to the level of humanity and *judging Him* by the way people treat us. As well, people who have been abused by a man will have a strong distrust or hatred toward the idea that Jesus is a man, concluding that He cannot be trusted. The same is true for God the Father. There isn't usually a strong male identity attached to the Holy Spirit.

People of authority—especially pastors, teachers, and other adult Christians—may also influence what we believe about God. We oftentimes judge God by the way people in the church act. For example, we are taught in the Bible that it is wrong to gossip. When Christians are caught gossiping, their hypocritical actions speak volumes about the integrity of God and His Word.

Satan wants people to think that God and Jesus are critical, judgmental, and mean. When a Christian uses the "God card" to bring condemnation, shame, judgment, criticism, or correction, they are misrepresenting His character, trying to control and manipulate another person. For example, a pastor may intentionally shame a church member in front of the congregation to bring them into correction. In the same way, a parent may scold a child by telling them that God or Jesus would be ashamed of their behavior. This sends a strong message to the one being shamed that God sees them as shameful, and as a result, they'll have trouble believing God wants anything to do with them.

Sometimes a person chooses to make unhealthy choices and needs to be redirected. However, it's wrong to use the Scriptures out of context and apply them to situations to accomplish *your* goal. For example, a parent may misuse their parental authority over their child by *seriously overloading* a child with work and responsibility, treating them like slaves, or adding physical punishment if they don't obey. If the child starts to complain, the parent may quote this Scripture, Ephesians 6:1: "Children obey your parents in the Lord, for this is right." They're trying to convince the child that this is God's will and they have no say. This misuse of Scripture, taken out of context, doesn't honor the Lord and His Word. The person receiving this kind of treatment will feel manipulated and controlled and may, as a result, develop a hatred for the Lord and the Bible.

Many times, these negative beliefs about God arise while experiencing repeated trauma and begging and pleading for God to intervene and make it stop. But often it doesn't stop in a timely manner, especially in cases of physical and sexual abuse. The person might believe that Jesus sat and watched it happen and didn't care about them. When the abuse is repeated over and over, it's possible for a person to lose hope. All trust in God may be lost.

Other times, these negative beliefs about God arise when you've prayed and prayed about troubling situations in your life, and nothing seems to change. For example, you may be praying for healing that doesn't happen, or praying for a wayward child who doesn't come home. It's easy in these moments to lose all hope and believe God isn't involved, is distant, and possibly may not even care. This is a result of trying to explain and justify *why* things didn't happen the way you hoped they would. You may want to blame God so you can have an answer to the "why." This place is a slippery slope. If you're not careful, you will play right into the enemy's hands and get offended at God. You'll doubt His love for you, not trusting His good will and kindness toward you, and will start distancing yourself from Him in offense.

You must be honest with yourself concerning what you believe about God, no matter how bad it may sound. He already knows what you believe and wants you to know Him for who He really is. We don't always realize God has emotions and a character that is perfect and holy. He wants us to know the truth. Negative beliefs about God will keep you from having a successful Value Exchange.

> We don't always realize God has emotions and a character that is perfect and holy. He wants us to know the truth.

The goal of mind renewal is to align our mind with the mind of Christ, removing the conflict between us and God.

Remember that God is on your side. He loves you and wants you to succeed. You don't want to fall for the enemy's lies and become distanced from God, *the* source of love and life.

> **"For I know the plans and thoughts that I have for you,"**
> **says the Lord, "plans for peace and well-being and not**
> **for disaster, to give you a future and a hope."**
> *~Jeremiah 29:11* (AMP)

When addressing your negative beliefs about God, you must determine exactly what you believe. What is your God statement? An example of a God statement might be, "I believe that God doesn't care about me." This belief explains why "He didn't protect me and allowed the bad thing to happen to me."

The coping mechanisms you might use to deal with this belief are the following:

"GOD DOESN'T CARE ABOUT ME."

1. **Self-protection:** By not expecting Him to care about me, I won't be hurt or disappointed when something bad happens or He doesn't "show up."

2. **Self-protection:** Being angry with God keeps Him pushed away at a "safe" distance. I can ignore God and not have anything to do with Him or religion. By doing this, He won't have the power to hurt me anymore.

3. **Self-protection:** I can avoid situations that carry the risk of being hurt. For instance, it might motivate me NOT to do a Value Exchange because I don't trust Him to answer or protect me.

4. **Self-protection:** I can stay disappointed and hopeless so I won't get my "hopes dashed" and face another "letdown" and disappointment. By not expecting Him to care, I won't be hurt again.

5. **Self-motivation:** Because I do NOT expect Him to be involved, I must take care of all the details of my life by myself. "I'm all alone. I'm on my own. It's up to me."

6. **Self-promoting/elevation:** Holding God in contempt feels powerful and "gives me the upper hand" and "control" in the relationship.

7. **Self-comfort:** I can stay in this sad place to bring comfort. "It feels good to feel bad."

8. **Self-justice:** Holding God in contempt feels good because it's what He "deserves." If God doesn't care about me, then I don't have to care about Him.

9. **Self-elevating/comfort:** "I have the right to be sad." By letting everybody know how sad I am, I'll draw lots of attention and comfort from other people. This can become a manipulative tool.

After reading the list above, can you relate to any of these coping mechanisms you may be using? Do you understand the value of each coping mechanism? If so, are you willing to give them to Jesus and trust Him to give you something of Kingdom value? If there is resistance to letting your value go, then go to the end of Chapter 1 on how to break through it.

A Value Exchange may look like this:

> *Lord Jesus, I recognize I've believed, "You don't care about me." I have used the coping mechanisms (as above) for self-protection, self-motivation, self-elevation, self-comfort, and self-justice (or other). I ask Your forgiveness for doing this. I now choose to break agreement with the belief that "You don't care about me." I give up all these coping mechanisms and their value. I command all demonic assignments that have come against me because of this to go now, in Jesus' name. Lord Jesus, please clean this place out for me and give to me what You value in exchange.*

Be sure to take time to receive from the Lord.

After doing this exchange, make sure this belief no longer feels true. Ask yourself, "How do I feel about God right now?" Go back into the situation from the past and see how you feel about God back then as well. Does the negative belief still feel true?

> **Be sober (well balanced and self-disciplined), be alert and cautious at all times. That enemy of yours, the devil, prowls around like a roaring lion (fiercely hungry), seeking someone to devour.**
> *~1 Peter 5:8* [AMP]

For some people, doing a Value Exchange may be very intimidating. You may feel like you won't hear from the Lord. If you're feeling this way, some good questions to ask yourself would be, "Am I believing something negative about God or His character? Do I believe God loves me? Do I believe God is mean, judgmental, or waiting to punish me, etc.? Am I believing that God won't talk to me? If He did talk to me, do I feel like I would hear Him?"

Remember that God speaks to us in many ways. He knows how to communicate His heart to us. He may communicate using a picture, a Scripture verse, a memory, a thought, a feeling (like peace), a new perspective, or any number of ways unique to you. You may just feel better. The more we get Him out of the box, the better! Don't put an expectation on what you think He will say or do. Just relax and receive from Him in whatever way He chooses to communicate with you.

For example, your father may have been harsh to you as a child. As a result, you may believe God is mean, cold, and harsh. You might feel like God doesn't have anything positive to say to you. And so, you believe hearing a word from Him would be hurtful. The belief that you can't hear from Him may be your way to avoid doing a Value Exchange, which would protect you from being hurt by what He says.

The belief that God is mean, cold, and harsh may also make you believe He won't speak to you while giving you an exchange. This may cause you to avoid even trying to do a Value Exchange with Him. Or if you do try, believing that you won't hear from Him will protect you from being disappointed when you feel like you didn't receive anything. You may conclude, without even trying, that the Value Exchange just "doesn't work" for you!

> **Therefore the LORD longs to be gracious to you, and therefore He waits on high to have compassion on you. For the LORD is a God of justice; How blessed are all those who long for Him.**
> *~Isaiah 30:18* (NASB)

Possible coping mechanisms attached to this belief might be the following:

"I CAN'T OR WON'T HEAR FROM GOD IN A VALUE EXCHANGE."

1. **Self-protection:** I don't expect to hear anything from God so I'm not going to be disappointed when He doesn't communicate with me. By doing this, I've put up a wall between myself and the Lord so He can't hurt me.

2. **Self-protection:** I avoid doing Value Exchanges because I believe He won't say anything good about me.

3. **Self-motivation:** I avoid communicating with God at all. I'm not even motivated to read the Bible anymore or go to church.

4. **Self-motivation:** I try harder to hear God by attending more church services, teaching Sunday School, etc.

5. **Self-elevation:** I look down on God, judging Him in disgust so that I'll feel more powerful and better about myself. "If I were God, I would have done things differently."

6. **Self-comfort:** I can feel sorry for myself in this sad condition.

7. **Self-justice:** I build a case against God because He's not fair, according to my standards. Keeping Him "guilty" feels like taking justice.

If you identify with some of the above thoughts/beliefs AND you're willing to give up the coping mechanisms, you would pray the following:

Value Exchange:

Lord Jesus, I recognize I've compared you to my earthly parent (by believing that You are cold, harsh, and mean) and have believed that I won't hear from You (even with a Value Exchange). I've built a wall of mistrust between myself and You, blocking myself from hearing You to protect myself from being hurt by You. I've motivated myself to avoid seeking You by not reading my Bible or going to church. I'm sorry and ask Your forgiveness for doing this. I now choose to break agreement with the belief that I can't or won't hear from You (in a Value Exchange). I give up all the ungodly benefits of protection and motivation. I command that all demonic assignments connected to this must go, in Jesus' name! Lord Jesus, I ask that You clean this place out for me and give to me what You value in exchange.

Be sure to take time to receive from the Lord.

After doing this exchange, make sure that this belief no longer feels true. Ask yourself, "How do I feel about hearing from God now?" Does it still feel true that God won't speak to me? Does it still feel true that He is mean, cold, and harsh?

Prayer:

Holy Spirit, I ask that You draw my heart into the truth of God's character; that I would not judge Him by what my eyes see or by what I'm feeling. Shed light on all my objections, Lord. Expose my wrong thinking. Open me up to Your truth. Oh God, fill me with the expectation of Your faithfulness. Increase my understanding of Your intentions toward me. Help me to know, without doubt, that You are good. Increase my hunger to know You as the lover of my heart. Oh God, I thank You for the Holy Spirit. I love how He draws me to You. Thank You, Jesus, that You are faithful.

CHAPTER 4

DOUBT

Doubt is the opposite of faith. Related to God, doubt is *not being convinced* that what He says is true. Doubt also questions His motives. Synonyms for doubt include distrust, suspicion, disbelief, hesitancy, wavering and questioning. These words are pretty harsh. When doubt comes between us and God, we will question His character and good intentions for our lives. His promises of joy and the "peace that passes understanding" (Philippians 4:6) feel like a joke.

The enemy has an arsenal of evidence to PROVE GOD WRONG. When things don't turn out like we thought they would, we question the wisdom and character of God. We think we know "better," and we would have done things differently! This part of our mind thinks more logically, and we doubt. This is what we call double-minded—part of our mind believes Him and the other part struggles with how to think because of the "case" built against Him.

In the Bible, we first see doubt show up in the garden of Eden when the serpent's questions caused Adam and Eve to doubt God's character and goodness (Genesis 3:1-5). The serpent masqueraded as a friendly, helpful voice and was able to put doubt in Eve's mind, causing her to question whether God would carry through on His rules (that the consequence would be death) and convincing her that God was withholding from her, not having her best interests in mind. Therefore, she decided to eat the fruit from the tree.

Because he is a master liar and deceiver, Satan is still able to speak into our minds today and we don't even realize he's speaking. We think his thoughts are our own. His goal is to get us to *agree* with him and to pervert God's character by causing us to believe He doesn't love us, is not faithful, is a liar, etc. Our agreement with Satan allows his dark kingdom access into our world, enabling him to "steal, kill and destroy" (John 10:10).

> IF YOU CHOOSE TO RELY ON YOURSELF RATHER THAN GOD, YOU'RE SETTING YOURSELF UP FOR FAILURE AND HARDSHIP. THE ENEMY IS MORE THAN HAPPY TO ASSIST YOU IN YOUR EFFORTS!

Doubt is a trust issue. We may doubt that God cares or loves us when we go through trials and He doesn't appear to show up. We then feel unprotected and unloved, and He feels distant and uncaring. Therefore, we don't trust Him to lead us through trials or that He will "cause all things to work together for good" (Romans 8:28). If we can't see that God is working in our situation, then we'll want to step in, figure it out, and take control into our own hands. In this way, doubt helps us to feel more in control.

You must decide—you're either going to trust God "no matter what" or attach coping mechanisms to help you navigate through the trial. This is a good time to remember the fact that GOD IS THE SOURCE AND POWER OF LOVE AND EVERYTHING GOOD IN THE WORLD! The power of darkness is present as well, coming against the good plans of God in your life. There IS a spiritual realm actively involved in our lives—and we can't defeat the enemy in that realm without God's wisdom and abilities. If you choose to rely on yourself rather than God, you're setting yourself up for failure and hardship. The enemy is more than happy to assist you in your efforts!

We can live in denial that this invisible realm exists, deciding to maneuver through life on our own. But, Jesus died to give you the Holy Spirit as a companion and guide, connecting you to His Father and Himself. Holy Spirit is also your connection to Heaven, where you are seated in the heavenly places in Christ. The degree to which you live out that reality is the degree to which you deepen in your relationship with the Lord, trusting Him and, by faith, obeying His directions.

When you're in the middle of a trial, feeling hopeless and unable to see any way out, will you allow yourself to trust Him to help? Will you trust Him to communicate with you and help you get through? You may want an instant solution, but will you wait on Him to work things out for you? Waiting tests your patience and ability to endure (James 1:3-4), but also strengthens your relationship with Him. He really CAN be your source of protection, motivation, comfort, elevation and justice. With The Value Exchange, you're giving up your old "self" coping mechanisms and allowing Him to help.

Example 1: Doubt sometimes shows up when doing a Value Exchange. You may feel like your current situation will never change and that doing an exchange won't help. The intensity of the bad emotions may be so strong and the circumstances surrounding the trial so convincing that it's hard to see how it would even be possible for God to work things out for your good. If you can't "see" it, you can't trust God to bring it about. Doubt helps you think a certain way that prepares you for the future and keeps you from being disappointed if nothing changes.

If you're ready to put your trust in His provision for you, a Value Exchange may sound like this:

> *Lord Jesus, I recognize I have come into agreement with doubt and have used it to protect me from being disappointed. I ask Your forgiveness for doing this. I now choose to break agreement with doubt and to give up its ungodly protection. I command all demonic assignments that have come against me because of this to go now, in Jesus' name! Lord Jesus, I ask you to clean this out for me and give me what You have in exchange.*

Be sure to take time to receive from the Lord.

After saying this prayer, ask yourself if you can trust the Lord now. Does it still feel true that doing a Value Exchanges won't help? If so, there may be another benefit (coping mechanism) connected to the doubt. Also ask yourself if there is any resistance in breaking agreement with doubt and its protection. If so, then go to the end of Chapter 1 that deals with resistance.

Example 2: Even if you do trust the Lord and make a Value Exchange, you may not believe the results will *last*. For example, you may feel good in the moment of the Value Exchange but afterwards be a little fearful, thinking "I hope it lasts." The peace and truth are there now. Why wouldn't they last? Doubt creeps in because you've never had peace that persists and surpasses understanding. You don't have a grid for that kind of life. You may only tend to trust and believe in what you've already experienced because it's been proven true and possible to you. That's the way our brains work! And the enemy is quite happy to poke you again and prove to you it didn't work. Because the poke is an emotion, it feels true. But after the Value Exchange, you need to stand in your healing and command doubt to go! The value you place on listening to doubt in this situation is to protect you from being disappointed if the healing from the Value Exchange doesn't last.

A Value Exchange may sound like this:

> *Lord Jesus, I recognize that I've come into agreement with doubt, believing the Value Exchange won't last. I've used doubt to protect myself from being disappointed. I ask Your forgiveness for doing this. I now choose to break agreement with doubt and to give up its ungodly protection. I command all demonic assignments that have come against me because of this to go now, in Jesus' name! Lord Jesus, I ask you to clean this out for me and give me what You have in exchange.*

Be sure to take time to receive from the Lord.

Ask yourself if it still feels true that a Value Exchange won't last. If it no longer feels true and you feel confident in moving forward doing exchanges, then you're all set! If not, there may be a coping mechanism attached to doubt that you missed. Or you may need to address any resistance you felt during the prayer.

We like to be in control. We think that *if we're in control* then we can "guarantee" all things will "work out for our good." We'll find a way to make sure we don't get hurt or disappointed. Doubt will give us plans to avoid pain or a bad outcome and may seem like the *wise* thing to do. If we're only half expecting something good to happen, then doubt will give us other ideas, like Plan B or Plan C—in case Plan A (God showing up) doesn't work.

The harder the trial, the harder it is to trust God in it. The length of the trial is another factor leading to doubt. Some trials go on for years. We let the trial determine how we think and are often beaten up and taken captive by it, rather than standing firm in what we know to be true about God's heart for us.

What does the Plan A of God "showing up" look like? It's trusting that He has a plan even though you don't know what it is. He is asking you to trust Him to walk you through the trial step by step, allowing Him to engage you at a heart level by letting Him care for your heart through it. He helps you know how to think, stand, keep your peace "in spite of," and know how to pray—to support you so you don't get beaten up and taken captive. This is not a place of inactivity. But it *is* a place, in your weakness, to stand on Kingdom principles and lean into His strength.

> What does the Plan A of God "showing up" look like? It's trusting that He has a plan even though you don't know what it is. He is asking you to trust Him to walk you through the trial step by step, allowing Him to engage you at a heart level by letting Him care for your heart through it.

> **Consider it nothing but joy, my brothers and sisters,
> whenever you fall into various trials. Be assured that
> the testing of your faith (through experience) produces
> endurance (leading to spiritual maturity, and inner
> peace). And let endurance have its perfect result and
> do a thorough work, so that you may be perfect and
> completely developed (in your faith), lacking in nothing.**
> *~James 1:2-3* (AMP)

What are your thoughts about the first sentence of this verse? How does it make you feel that God would test your faith? Do you see His plan for you in the testing? Sometimes God's Plan A doesn't make sense to our reasoning. He often will take you on a path that doesn't make sense. Can you trust and understand that His heart is to grow you and not destroy you in the testing? He has intentional plans to weed out everything that opposes His truth so you can stand in any storm and not be shaken (Hebrews 12:27).

By having a Plan B and Plan C, we are double-minded, believing in Him and having plans of our own "just in case." For example, you may be praying for financial breakthrough but you're not trusting His leading to take a job that you don't think will supply your needs. At this point, it's necessary to ask God for His wisdom and trust Him to give it to you.

> **If any of you lacks wisdom (to guide him through a decision
> or circumstance), he is to ask of (our benevolent) God, who
> gives to everyone generously and without rebuke or blame, and
> it will be given to him. But he must ask (for wisdom) in faith,
> *without doubting* (God's willingness to help), for the one who
> doubts is like a billowing surge of the sea that is blown about
> and tossed by the wind. For such a person ought not to think
> or expect that he will receive anything (at all) from the Lord,
> being a double-minded man, unstable and restless in all his
> ways (in everything he thinks, feels, or decides).**
> *~James 1:5-8* (AMP)

He has the answers you need. Doubt questions God's wisdom. Sometimes trusting His wisdom and waiting on Him for these things seems irresponsible because nothing ever seems to change for the better. At some point, we give up on Him and take matters into our own hands. Sometimes the decisions we make come from exasperation and desperation, and we often choose unwise plans. In these examples, doubt becomes a motivator to come up with a plan, finding a way to make something happen.

We need to be convinced of His perfect character and completely trust Him in order to NOT DOUBT. We want to doubt God when we can't explain Him or we feel out of control. This "just in case" and "half expecting Him to show up" part of our mind compromises our relationship with the Lord.

We may get angry with God for not answering our prayers in the timing and way we think He should. If you feel angry with God, go to the God Issues chapter for healing.

A Value Exchange may sound like this:

> *Lord Jesus, I recognize that I've used doubt to motivate myself to do something about the situation so I can FEEL in control. In doing this, I also feel safer because it seems like I can guarantee the outcome. I'm not trusting You. I ask Your forgiveness for doing this. I now choose to break agreement with doubt and give up its motivation and control. I command all demonic assignments connected to this to go, in Jesus' name! Lord Jesus, I ask You to clean this out and give me what You have in exchange.*

Be sure to take time to receive from the Lord.

Go to a memory where you felt doubt and the need to be in control. How does that feel now? How do you feel about that situation? What feels true to you now? If you still feel the need to doubt, then you need to look for other possible coping mechanisms attached to it or possibly address another God issue.

Possible coping mechanisms related to doubt are the following:

1. **Self-protection:** By being double minded, I protect myself from being disappointed. I don't want to hope for something that won't happen.

2. **Self-protection:** Protects me from looking like a fool. Because of doubt, I may choose not to pray for someone to be healed because I "know" it won't work anyway and then I won't look bad. I don't want to take the risk.

3. **Self-protection:** Protects me from making a wrong decision.

4. **Self-motivation:** I now proactively look for my own solutions that I can count on (Plans B and C).

5. **Self-motivation:** Even if I've heard God clearly, I get other people's opinions to make sure "God is right."

6. **Self-justice:** I can feel justified holding onto doubt through a trial as a cautionary measure. The doubt says, "Aha! I told you so" when things don't go the way I thought they should.

Doubt is like a yellow light of caution that tells you to either slow down, partially believe, or stop believing in God's intimate involvement in your life. Doubt wants to replace God's wisdom with your own wisdom. Doubt puts a question in your mind, making you think the Bible's promises are not for you. They might be for other people, but you don't feel they're for YOU. And so you hesitate to trust them for yourself.

In contrast, faith is like a green light and tells you to GO! Move forward only with what the Lord says to do, trusting Him to give you a red light if you misunderstood His direction. Expect and confidently know that HE WILL SHOW UP! Trust in His character and His love for you. Give up control; throw away your own ideas and plans in exchange for His! He is faithful to keep His Word and not let you down.

> **For I am (actively) watching over My Word to fulfill it.**
> ~*Jeremiah 1:12* (AMP)

So will My Word which goes out of My mouth; It will not return to Me void (useless, without result), without accomplishing what I desire, and without succeeding in the matter for which I sent it.
~*Isaiah 55:11*[(AMP)]

Prayer:

Oh God, I so desire to "know You!" I want the "yada" connection with You. To truly know You would be that my heart is connected with Yours in unconditional love, and that my mind is willing to not seek my own self-motivations but to submit and seek Your will only in every aspect of my life! Thank you, Papa, that Your heart is to love me with a love that is purely motivated to bring me into a place of complete unity as "one" with You. Increase the capacity of my heart to love You more!

("Yada" definition [Hebrew]: "to know," "enter into covenant together")

CHAPTER 5

Identity Issues

Identity comes from what you believe about yourself. It is a complex process of developing a view about yourself that comes from an accumulation of experiences and interactions with other people. You look at your successes and failures, rating how well you succeed or fail compared to others. How you process this information, for good or for bad, *will* determine how you act and react in future situations.

In this process, you're developing your identity *without God's input*. Identity is often determined by what you *perceive* other people are thinking about you, based on how they treat you and what they say about you. You take it ALL in, trying to figure out who you are and what value you have. The negative seems to speak louder than the positive information. Because your identity is affected so much by the negative, you end up giving people who hurt you power to determine your worth and well-being.

Essentially, you subconsciously make lists of perceived truths about yourself, detailing what you ARE and what you ARE NOT. Sometimes it's difficult to identify these subconscious beliefs. Below are some common self-beliefs:

LIST OF WHAT "I AM NOT"
not smart enough
not good enough
not enough
I don't measure up
not valuable
not anointed enough
not worth loving
not strong enough
I don't have a voice
not worthy
not popular
not attractive

LIST OF WHAT "I AM"

inadequate

worthless (or worth-less)

failure

rejected

trashy (feeling dirty, cheap)

useless (not good for anything)

defective (something is wrong with me)/damaged goods

inferior (I don't measure up)

meaningless/useless

I don't matter

I don't fit in/I don't belong

inconsequential (I don't play an important part of anything)

lame/pathetic

good for nothing

despicable, contemptible

lowly

a victim

powerless/helpless

only good for sex (I feel like an object)

vile, debased, degraded, degenerate, wretched

stupid/dumb

unloved; not loveable (nobody loves me/nobody cares)

overlooked/overshadowed/forgotten/invisible

alone

an anxious person

When negative information about you *feels true,* then you might take that belief and attach it to your identity. There is *power* in people's words, their actions, and facial expressions. You assimilate this information into beliefs about yourself because, "*it just feels so true.*" When someone says something good about you, it doesn't matter because you have all this evidence that speaks much louder than the good just spoken. These beliefs hit your heart at a core level and are very convincing at the moment of the hit. These negative beliefs cloud your vision, and you will walk in a perceived false reality/identity, at some level.

Your heart is going to express itself in some way. Once you're convinced something is true, it's hard to dismiss. This wounded thinking becomes your truth and reality. The problem with all these "truths" is that God, your Creator, has not been given a voice to speak into your identity. You don't know how to give Him a voice. It's no wonder we need a brand-new life and identity, which can only be found in Christ.

> **Therefore, if anyone is in Christ (that is, grafted in, joined to Him by faith in Him as Savior), he is a new creature (reborn and renewed by the Holy Spirit); the old things (the previous moral and spiritual condition) have passed away. Behold, new things have come (because spiritual awakening brings a new life).**
> *~2 Corinthians 5:17* (AMP)

The enemy is a master of deception. In our woundedness, we use pride and judgment to attack one another. We act and react to each other out of our wounded thinking. The enemy will use the brokenness within us to wound other people. In this way, the enemy is empowered. We use this negative information coming at us as evidence, which then forms our identity.

Your life is transformed when you have an encounter with God and His words become your truth. You'll have a new outlook on life by establishing new "I am" beliefs about yourself that are God-inspired, Kingdom truths. As you do these exchanges, make a new list—inspired by God!

UNHEALTHY BEHAVIORS (COPING MECHANISMS):

1. **People-pleasing:** Your well-being is dependent on other people's opinions about you. You're motivated to *earn* approval, acceptance, and love.

2. **Obsessive-Compulsive Behavior:** You perform behaviors such as frequent handwashing and/or taking showers several times a day to feel clean due to sexual abuse and feeling dirty. Or you need to have everything perfectly in place to feel in control, etc.

3. **Spending money:** Might give you a sense of comfort, value and/or control.

4. **Addiction:** Brings comfort by numbing you or helping you to forget pain. It can also be a distraction, calm anxiety or give you something to do to avoid boredom.

5. **Fantasy:** An intentional escape from reality allows you to imagine things, making you feel better about yourself.

6. **Thrill seeking:** Living "on the edge" for the adrenaline rush, trying to get attention or to prove you can do anything.

7. **Self-harming:** Self-injury feels like it releases intense emotional pain. You often don't feel the pain of the cut. Seeing the blood flow brings a temporary release and may cause a feeling of euphoria. Sometimes it's used for self-punishment, a distraction from emotional pain, or to feel something other than numbness, or as a way to express emotional pain.

8. **Thoughts of suicide/suicide attempts:** These are ways of escaping emotional pain and unpleasant life situations. This can also be used to get attention or revenge.

9. **Perfectionism:** Performance behaviors have the goal of earning love, respect, acceptance and/or admiration. They are strong motivators that will push you to keep working harder but will never give you a break. The constant pushing effectively takes away your choice to take a break.

10. **Self-condemnation:** Looking at past failures, hurts and regrets will make you work harder to be better, making sure you don't make the same mistakes again.

Painful emotions like sadness, depression, and shame are attached to self-beliefs and become entrenched within us each time their message is repeated. The message carries the pain. Repetitive emotional and physical trauma accumulates and becomes a **stronghold**. A stronghold is a fortified place of security and survival. We think about the painful memory, with its negative emotions and beliefs, and then **connect** coping mechanisms to it. This helps us to know how to think, stay safe, and feel more in control of our lives. In this way, we develop habitual ways of thinking based upon the package of emotion/belief. The more the pain is reinforced, the stronger the stronghold becomes. We literally build our lives around the events that caused us so much pain. Therefore, we take actions on our own instead of trusting in God's protection.

The lies that feel so true become more important and appear more real than God's Word and His opinion about us. This develops into inner captivity and deception, which causes misery and defeat. This will keep a person from thinking clearly and accepting God's truth. As time goes by, the enemy will constantly poke and BUILD upon that initial lie, reinforcing it. The enemy is the master of deception. In this way, he robs us of our true, God-given identity in Christ.

EXAMPLES OF VALUE EXCHANGES:

1. I don't matter/rejection

As a little child, your parent promised (on many occasions) that you would spend time together, doing something fun. You remember sitting by the window waiting for them to get home from work only to find out AGAIN that they are "running late" and won't be able to keep those plans. This is very painful, and you start to believe, "I don't matter." Even as an adult, you continue to feel the pain of "I don't matter" when something you've planned with friends falls through.

What are some possible things you might do to cope with this belief?

1. **Self-protection:** I expect *not* to matter to someone, so I'm not hurt as badly when they let me down.

2. **Self-protection**: I subconsciously put up an emotional wall and distance myself from friends to protect myself from being hurt by them.

3. **Self-motivation/self-protection/self-elevation:** I motivate myself to try harder to succeed in relationships. I might be over-complimentary ("a brown-noser") or become a "people pleaser" to earn value and protect myself from being hurt or rejected.

4. **Self-elevation:** I put them down in my mind or openly to other people, which helps me to feel better about myself.

5. **Self-protection:** I use anger to push someone away or try to force them to treat me better.

6. **Self-justice:** I use anger to retaliate by canceling plans with them to take justice.

7. **Self-protection/self-elevation:** I put on an act, being overly dramatic and cheerful to get people's attention and earn value. This also tries to protect me from not mattering to that person.

8. **Self-protection:** I sabotage a potentially promising relationship before the other person has a chance to reject me.

9. **Self-justice:** I justify unforgiveness because of how they made me feel. If I let this go, then I would have to forgive them. They don't deserve it.

You get an understanding that the belief "I don't matter" caused you to put up an emotional wall to protect your heart from getting hurt. When you're willing to let go of that wall, your Value Exchange would look something like this:

Lord Jesus, I recognize that I've been holding onto the belief of "I don't matter" and have used this wall to protect my heart from being hurt again. I'm sorry and ask Your forgiveness for doing this. I now choose to break agreement with the belief that I don't matter, and I give up the way I'm using this wall to protect my heart. I command all demonic assignments that have come against me because of this to go, in Jesus' name! Lord Jesus, I ask that You clean this out for me and give to me what You value in exchange.

Be sure to take time to receive from the Lord.

Remember to go to a memory where you felt rejected or like you didn't matter. Does it still feel true that you don't matter? Do you still feel rejected? If this no longer feels true, you've gotten a successful Value Exchange. If either belief feels true, then search for any resistance or missed benefit. If the beliefs don't feel true, but there are other negative emotions still in the memory, address them next and do another Value Exchange.

2. Abandonment/alone

As a child, your parents got divorced. In the emotional turmoil they were going through, you felt neglected and all alone. As you grew up, you struggled with fear of abandonment and being alone. As an adult, you feel alone all the time, even when you're in a room full of people. You may have trouble trusting people. You could take up the mantra of, "I'm all alone. I'm on my own. It's up to me." In this way, you have made yourself responsible to take care of yourself.

What are some possible things you might do to cope with the feelings of being abandoned and alone?

1. **Self-motivation:** I do whatever it takes to not be alone, possibly clinging onto another person (which could turn into an ungodly soul tie).

2. **Self-protection:** I put up a wall so I don't get too close to someone and therefore won't be hurt by them if they abandon me.

3. **Self-protection**: I isolate myself from others because I know how to "be alone." This feels safer because it protects me from being abandoned.

4. **Self-comfort:** I find comfort in being alone, knowing there's no risk. Alone is my "comfort zone."

5. **Self-elevation:** Because I feel a friend has abandoned me, I gossip about them to make myself feel better by putting them down. I may not vocally put them down, but in my mind, I am doing it a lot in order to feel better about myself.

6. **Self-justice:** Because I felt abandoned by a friend, I'm justified when I choose not to forgive them. Not forgiving them feels like taking justice because they deserve it.

You get an understanding that you're using the feeling of being alone and abandoned to self-protect by isolating yourself from other people. If you're willing to give up the protection of isolation, your Value Exchange would look like this:

Lord Jesus, I recognize I've been holding onto the feeling of being abandoned and alone and am protecting myself by avoiding people. I'm sorry and ask Your forgiveness for doing this. I now choose to break agreement with using the feelings of being abandoned and alone and give up the value of avoidance for protection. I command all demonic assignments that have come against me because of this to go now, in Jesus' name! Lord Jesus, I ask that You clean this out for me and give to me what You value in exchange.

Be sure to take time to receive from the Lord.

Remember to go to a memory where you felt alone or abandoned. Do those emotions still feel true? If they no longer feel true, you've gotten a successful Value Exchange. If it still feels true, then search for any resistance or missed benefit. If the beliefs don't feel true, but there are other negative emotions still in the memory, address them next and do another Value Exchange.

3. Not good enough, failure, or inferior

As a college student, you have a lot of anxiety. You're under constant stress to get good grades and are now having anxiety attacks. You have problems focusing and can't sleep well at night. This would be a good time to ask yourself, "How would it make me feel if I didn't get a good grade on a test?" You recognize that if you didn't do well on a test, you would feel that you're "not good enough or a failure." As a child, you never felt like you did anything well enough for your parents. You thought they only pointed out what you did wrong instead of praising you for what you did right. In school, you found that getting good grades helped you feel better about yourself.

What are some possible things you might do to cope with the feeling of being "not good enough, failure or inferior"?

1. **Self-motivation:** I can use this belief as a positive motivator, pushing me to work harder and prove myself.

2. **Self-motivation:** I can use this belief as a negative motivator, which causes me to give up trying. Giving up is easier than trying so hard.

3. **Self-motivation:** I can use this belief to punish myself, which encourages me to try harder to do better.

4. **Self-protection:** This belief helps keep my guard up around my peers. I can also avoid being around my parents and other people who might make me feel "not good enough."

5. **Self-protection:** Believing "I'm not good enough" gives me an excuse to get out of things that seem too risky.

6. **Self-protection:** Knowing "I'm not good enough" pads the blow in situations when I'm around people who've made me feel that way before. If I already believe this, they can't make me feel any worse about myself than I already feel.

7. **Self-comfort:** I can use the sadness of feeling "not good enough" as self-pity, which gives me comfort.

8. **Self-justice:** I can take justice by punishing myself because I deserve it. This helps me to feel better.

9. **Self-elevation:** The belief causes me to do things to make myself look better to other people so I feel better about me. Doing this helps me feel like I have equal or greater value.

10. **Self-comfort/self-protection:** By knowing my place and value, I know what to expect from other people and how I fit into any situation. In this way, I can be comfortable with who I am.

By embracing the belief, "I'm not good enough," you are motivating yourself to work harder to protect yourself from getting hurt and to look good in other people's eyes. You are now willing to give this belief, along with its benefits of positive motivation, protection, and elevation, to Jesus in exchange for what He has for you. Your Value Exchange would be like this:

> *Lord Jesus, I recognize I've been holding onto the belief that I'm not good enough (or a failure/inferior) and I have used it to motivate myself to work harder, elevate myself, and to protect myself from being hurt. I'm sorry and ask Your forgiveness for doing this. I now choose to break agreement with the belief that I'm not good enough (or a failure) and give up all its motivation, elevation, and protection. I command all demonic assignments that have come against me because of this to go, in Jesus' name! Lord Jesus, I ask You to please clean this out for me and give me what You have in exchange.*

Be sure to take time to receive from the Lord.

Remember to go to a memory where you felt like you don't matter, like you are a failure or inferior. Do these beliefs still feel true? If they no longer feel true, you've gotten a successful Value Exchange. If they still feel true, then search for any resistance or missed benefit. If the beliefs don't feel true, but there are other negative emotions still in the memory, address them next and do another Value Exchange.

The beliefs of being not good enough and/or being a failure are commonly used as motivators to try harder and perform better. But at some point, these tools are not enough to get the job done. There is often a gradual progression of negative coping mechanisms. For example, adding anxiety to a negative self-belief as another coping mechanism would motivate you even more. By this time, many people are so used to the negative motivation of both "not good enough" and anxiety that they can't even imagine giving them up. They honestly believe they NEED these negative motivators to get things done. Without them, they may not make any effort at all. An additional Value Exchange would look like this:

Lord Jesus, I recognize I've used the belief that I'm not good enough, along with anxiety, to motivate myself to work harder. I ask Your forgiveness for doing this. I now choose to break agreement with using the feelings of "not good enough" and anxiety as a motivator and give up all their value. I command all demonic assignments connected to this to go now, in Jesus' name! Lord Jesus, I ask You to clean this out for me and give me what You value in exchange.

Be sure to take time to receive from the Lord.

Remember to go to a memory where you felt anxiety and not good enough. Does it still feel true that you're not good enough? Do you still feel anxiety? If not, you've gotten a successful Value Exchange. If either belief or emotion feels true, then search for any resistance or missed benefit.

4. Worthless/unloved

As a child, you weren't the favorite and received the brunt of your parents' anger and frustration while your siblings got the hugs and acceptance. This caused you to believe something was wrong with you and that you were not lovable. It also led to the belief that love is conditional and needs to be earned. Even though you're now an adult, you have trouble believing God loves you unconditionally. You work hard to be perfect by people-pleasing, hoping they'll value or love you.

What are some possible things you might do to cope with the feeling of being worthless and unloved?

1. **Self-protection:** I keep people pushed away to prevent them from getting too close to my heart.

2. **Self-motivator/protector:** People-pleasing is a way to earn love, respect, and keep people from disapproving of me.

3. **Self-motivation/manipulation and control:** Feeling unloved and worthless motivates me to find a way to feel loved and valued. I may do this by putting expectations on people to treat me in ways I've determined love should look and feel like. People close to me need to meet my love language or it doesn't feel like love to me. By doing this, I'm putting a demand on love. For example, proof

of love to me might be expecting constant affirmation or acts of service.

4. **Self-motivation:** I look for signs of not being loved (overthinking). I start to notice every single thing, in any remote way, that might confirm my suspicions. In doing this, I become hyperaware.

5. **Self-protection:** By staying on high alert, I will look for signs of possible rejection and then choose to reject someone before they can reject me.

6. **Self-justice**: By holding anger against my parents or whoever hurt me, I can punish them by pushing them out of my life. I feel justified because they don't deserve to be part of my life.

7. **Self-comfort**: I will hold sadness to bring comfort to myself (self-pity). Other people will feel sorry for me and I'll get their attention.

In the example above, you get an understanding that you're trying to earn love and acceptance by pleasing people. This also protects you from their disapproval. Your Value Exchange might look like this:

Lord Jesus, I recognize I've been holding onto the belief that I'm worthless/unloved and have used it to motivate myself to work harder to earn love. I've used it to protect myself from disapproval. I'm sorry and ask Your forgiveness for doing this. I now choose to break agreement with worthless/unloved and give up its motivation to earn love and people-pleasing. I command all demonic assignments that have come against me because of this to go, in Jesus' name! Lord Jesus, I ask You to clean this out for me and give me what You have in exchange.

Be sure to take time to receive from the Lord.

After doing this exchange, make sure this belief no longer feels true. Ask yourself, "Do I still feel worthless or unloved?" Go back into the memory from the past and see how you feel about yourself there. Does the negative belief still feel true? If so, then you need to look for a possible attached coping mechanism you missed.

5. Who holds the power over your well-being?

You recognize that certain people have a great amount of influence over your identity and well-being. This could be anyone from the past or current relationships. Deep inside, you're allowing your wounded feelings to determine your truth. You've given the very people who hurt you the power to determine your value, which in turn, affects your well-being.

What do you believe about yourself because of them?

Pause right now and make a list.

_____

_____

_____

The reason you believe these things is that your subconscious mind automatically attempts to make sense of the information coming in, helping you know how to think, how to be, and act accordingly. This is all done to earn love, favor, and to feel safe. This is called the fear of man.

> **The fear of man brings a snare, But whoever trusts in and puts his confidence in the Lord will be exalted and safe.**
> ~*Proverbs 29:25* (AMP)

To break agreement with the fear of man and the power you've given this person(s) to determine your well-being, pray the following:

Lord Jesus, I recognize that I've given _____
power over my well-being. I've allowed them to determine my value and speak into my identity in a negative way by believing _____
_____ *(list could contain multiple beliefs). I've done this to help me know how to think and how to act to earn love, favor, and keep my heart safe. I'm sorry and ask Your forgiveness for doing this. I also choose to forgive them for hurting*

me. I choose to break agreement with the fear of man and give up all its ungodly benefits. I choose to take the power over my well-being out of their hands, and I put it back into Your hands where it belongs. I command all demonic assignments connected to the fear of man to go now, in Jesus' name! Lord Jesus, I ask You to clean this place out for me and fill it with what You have in exchange.

Be sure to take time to receive from the Lord.

After doing this exchange, you want to put yourself back into a memory where you felt that negative feeling and see if it feels any different. Does the negative belief still feel true? How do you feel about that person now? Do they still have power over you? Do you feel like you have forgiven them?

In some cases, there could be an ungodly soul tie present that also needs to be broken. A possible clue of this is when your well-being is dependent on someone else's well-being. You can only be at peace when someone else is happy or approving of you. See the chapter on Soul Ties.

> **But to as many as did receive and welcome Him, He gave the right (the authority, the privilege) to become children of God, that is, to those who believe in (adhere to, trust in, and rely on) His name – who were born, not of blood (natural conception), nor of the will of the flesh (physical impulse), nor of the will of man (that of a natural father), but of God (that is, a divine and supernatural birth—they are born of God—spiritually transformed, renewed, sanctified).**
> *~John 1:12-13* (AMP)

By doing value exchanges regarding your identity, you receive from God a new, Kingdom-inspired list detailing the truth of who you are and who you are not. In this way, how you view yourself and act accordingly will align with the righteousness of God and who He created you to be. You must become aware of your thought life. What you believe, you will empower and manifest. You will be what you believe (Proverbs 23:7)! You ARE a reborn child of God with a new identity in Christ!

Prayer:

I praise You, Jesus, and I thank You for Your redemptive power. The power to transform my life of pain and sorrow into a life that sings Your praises. I thank You for Your pure, Holy Love that penetrates my very being and purifies me, restores me, and fills me with peace and joy! Your presence is what I long for and I cannot get enough of You.

CHAPTER 6

THE MANY FACES OF FEAR
Anxiety, Stress and Worry

Fear is the expectation that something bad is going to happen. A variety of things can trigger fear. For example, fear can come from having something bad happen or from watching the news or a scary movie. As a result, your heart may pound, your hands shake, and you start to sweat. Once present, fear can be hard to let go of. Fear will cause you to remember, gaze at, and fixate your thoughts on things you fear. This will cause anxiety, stress, and worry. You begin to be vigilant, looking for things that could possibly harm you. In this way, fear becomes your protector!

At the time of this writing, the world is dealing with the risk of getting an infection with Covid and whether to get the vaccine. There are risks with both. Fear wants to help you decide which risk to choose. When you make a decision out of fear, it is likely to be the wrong one, for the wrong reasons.

There are multiple and various opportunities to embrace fear. If you can't think of anything to fear, someone else will be happy to introduce you to their fears! What are good friends for, but to help you see what possible horrible things might be awaiting you around the corner! The escalation of fear might look something like this: When you have an unexplained pain that's probably a pulled muscle, your good friend informs you about a "friend of a friend" with a similar pain who had a heart attack. Instantly you feel fear, now believing the pain is dangerous and you could die at any moment. Now, you're under the influence of fear.

The influence of your friend's fear will CAUSE you to react in a way to cope with this new information. First, you start to worry because you suddenly remember your uncle died of a heart attack and conclude it must run in the family. By worrying, you start to develop a case that justifies why the fear is valid. This all happens subconsciously as your mind tries to make sense of all the information you're accumulating. The physical pain is so magnified that it feels worse than when you first noticed it. You are now beginning to feel stressed. To gain control, stress and fear work to keep you more aware and alert of any physical pain so you don't miss anything and have something bad happen to you. This helps you feel more in control of the situation.

You start to lose sleep and begin talking about it to other people. You research the internet for every bit of information about heart attacks. Initially, you may hesitate to call your doctor, fearing it might be true that you have heart disease! Eventually, you give in and make an appointment to see your doctor. In reality, this anxiety is taking a toll on your body—it is actually causing you harm. To do a Value Exchange for worry, you must first figure out the value attached to it. How are you using worry to help you cope during this ordeal?

COPING MECHANISMS RELATED TO WORRY, STRESS, ANXIETY, AND FEAR:

1. **Self-protection:** Gets me ready for the bad news and how traumatizing and horrible that will make me feel. I won't be caught off guard. It will make me feel more in control because "I knew that could happen."

2. **Self-motivation:** I might research possible causes for the pain and/ or talk to other people to get their opinions.

3. **Self-elevation**: I'll draw attention to myself and get other people worried and concerned about me.

4. **Self-comfort**: It feels so good to worry sometimes. It makes me feel like I'm taking good care of myself. The attention I receive from others is reassuring and helps me feel cared for.

A Value Exchange might look like this:

Lord Jesus, I recognize I've been using worry/stress/anxiety/fear to feel more in control of the situation and to motivate me to take action and try to figure things out. I'm sorry and ask Your forgiveness for doing this. I now choose to break agreement with worry/stress/anxiety/fear and give up all its protection and motivation. I command all demonic assignments connected to this to go, in Jesus' name! Lord Jesus, I ask You to please clean this place out for me and give to me what You have in exchange.

Be sure to take time to receive from the Lord.

After doing this exchange, check for the feelings of worry, stress, anxiety, and/or fear in a memory. How are you responding to whatever you were worrying about? Are you still feeling worried, stressed, anxious, or fearful? If so, then you need to look for another possible coping mechanism you may have missed.

Do not be anxious or worried about anything, but in everything (every circumstance and situation) by prayer and petition with thanksgiving, continue to make your (specific) requests known to God. And the peace of God (that peace which reassures the heart, that peace) which transcends all understanding, (that peace which) stands guard over your hearts and your minds in Christ Jesus (is yours).
~Philippians 4:6-7 (AMP)

Another common example of worry is how a parent or grandparent worries about their children's or grandchildren's well-being and safety. Worry is a socially acceptable way to show concern. For example, when I tell people, "I don't worry about my kids," they look at me as though something is wrong with me and presume that I must not care about them. Finding out someone is worrying about you can feel good and proves they must really care. However, worry is actually allowing your mind to dwell on negative things and how you might prevent bad things from happening. This is a mindset of negative thinking. This mindset is not from the Lord. He is not a negative thinker.

The undercurrent of worry keeps your mind busy trying to figure out solutions and how you will respond to any situation. You may feel like you're organizing information, reassuring yourself about it to feel more in control. Even though nothing is being accomplished, just thinking about things gives your subconscious mind something to do in situations you have no control over. This can help you feel more in control! You can try to control other people's behavior, like your children, so that you can worry less. The worry may also feel like wisdom when you're giving your loved one a heads-up warning to avoid bad things from happening. You might feel like the worry keeps you and your loved one safer and more prepared.

In reality, you're attempting to use worry to give you a sense of control over your future and that of your loved ones rather than giving God control, trusting and resting in Him.

A Value Exchange might look like this:

> *Lord Jesus, I recognize I've taken on worry as a way to feel more in control of life's situations that are out of my control. I've used it like wisdom and to protect my heart from being hurt. I've used it to help my heart feel better because I'm showing that I care. I'm sorry and ask Your forgiveness for doing this. I now choose to break agreement with worry and I give up all its value. I command all demonic assignments connected to this to go, in Jesus' name! Lord Jesus, I ask You to please clean this place out and give me what You have in exchange.*

Be sure to take time to receive from the Lord.

After doing this exchange, remember to make sure that the feeling of worry and out of control are gone. Do you still feel the same about the situations you were worrying about? What's your perspective now about those concerns?

Fear and anxiety are powerful influencers that will cause you to respond and take some type of action, affecting your decisions and responses. The same situation could be viewed from the perspective of peace and wisdom, but you can't see clearly due to the presence of fear.

Peace is a state that is free from anxiety or distress. It's an emotional state of tranquility and calmness. Wisdom is the ability to make sensible decisions. A given situation will look different depending on whether it's being evaluated from the viewpoint of fear or from peace and wisdom. For example, even our prayers will sound a lot different if they're spoken from a place of peace and rest instead of motivated by fear. The prayers will be confident, expecting God's intervention, when they come from a place of peace. The prayer will sound more like begging and pleading when fear is present.

For example, let's say you're feeling fearful about an issue and would like to pray to the Lord about it in peace. Below are listed some possible coping mechanisms connected to fear and how they influence the way you pray.

> The undercurrent of worry keeps your mind busy trying to figure out solutions and how you will respond to any situation. You may feel like you're organizing information, reassuring yourself about it to feel more in control. Even though nothing is being accomplished, just thinking about things gives your subconscious mind something to do in situations you have no control over. This can help you feel more in control!

COPING MECHANISMS ATTACHED TO FEAR:

1. **Self-motivation/self-protection:** I will pray loudly, begging and pleading with God to get His attention and change the situation so the bad thing won't happen.

2. **Self-motivation:** I will pray more often, and fervently, and try to get others to pray. It might motivate me to promise to go to church every Sunday or stop a bad habit.

3. **Self-comfort:** Praying harder, longer, louder, and more often, along with stirring others to pray, gives me comfort about the situation.

By praying with the wrong motivation of fear, you're trying to control the situation and God, rather than trusting Him. Fear makes you forget that God has an answer to the problem. When you pray from a place of peace and trust, you access God's Kingdom solution for the problem. You then are able to pray God's will into the circumstances.

> **"So, do not be like them (praying as they do); for your
> Father knows what you need before you ask Him.
> Pray, then, in this way: 'Our Father who is in heaven,
> Hallowed be Your name. Your Kingdom come, Your
> will be done On earth as it is in heaven."**
> *~Matthew 6:8-10* (AMP)

A possible Value Exchange might sound like this:

Jesus, I recognize I've been using fear to motivate me to pray more often and with more emotion so that I'll be protected from bad things happening, which also brings me comfort. I'm sorry and ask for Your forgiveness. I now choose to break agreement with fear and to give up all the ways I've used it. I command all demonic assignments attached to these things to go now, in Jesus' name! Lord Jesus, I ask You to clean this out for me and give to me what You have in exchange.

Be sure to take time to receive from the Lord.

After doing this exchange, be sure you no longer feel fear. When you think about praying, what is your perspective and motivation now? You should feel peace and be motivated to pray out of love and compassion.

The Word of God has a lot to say about fear and anxiety. Repeatedly, it tells us not to fear or be anxious. Our perfect example is Jesus who never lived in fear. In a storm, He was sleeping in the boat while the disciples were scared for their lives! He didn't fear what people thought of Him either. He didn't fear a demoniac who was able to break through chains and was violent. He never had performance anxiety or believed He wasn't good enough or that He wouldn't get things right. After all, He was the Messiah, which would have to be a pretty stressful responsibility, right? He didn't fear rejection, even though He was rejected. We fear things that are immediate threats (like flying in a plane) but also fear what people think about us. We fear being rejected or looked down on or looking stupid. The list of things to fear goes on and on.

How did He do it? How did He not entertain fear? He walked in peace and wisdom all the time, which is the direct opposite of fear and anxiety. He knew His identity and the character of His Father. Because of this, He was able to walk out His perfect life as the Son of God.

> **Suddenly a violent storm developed, with waves so high the boat was about to be swamped. Yet Jesus continued to sleep soundly. The disciples woke Him up saying, "Save us, Lord! We're going to die!" But Jesus reprimanded them. "Why are you gripped with fear? Where is your faith?" Then He rebuked the storm and said, "Be still!" And instantly it became perfectly calm.**
> *~Matthew 8:24-26* (TPT)

There is a kind of fear that's healthy and is a natural built-in response to a dangerous situation. For example, fear is useful when you're driving in traffic and need to respond quickly to avoid hitting a person who suddenly walks in front of your car. Fear is helpful when you've gotten too close to the edge of a cliff and need to move back quickly.

Fear becomes unhealthy when you *HOLD ONTO* the feeling of fear, using IT to be more proactive in avoiding situations again. For example, if you're involved in a motor vehicle collision that was very frightening, you may subconsciously hold onto the fear of the accident, using it to help you fearfully drive more carefully, in a tensed-up state. Fear may become so empowered that you eventually stop driving.

Initial fear is natural and normal. But when we hold onto that fear, using it as a motivator to navigate situations, then it is actually replacing the wisdom and peace of God to guide us. Fear from the initial traumatic experience needs to be *RELEASED, otherwise it could become a stronghold.* Unfortunately, the subconscious mind brings it out again, using it in any perceived potentially dangerous situation to help you feel safer and more cautious. Jesus, the Prince of Peace, will keep in perfect peace all who trust in Him. His peace is only one Value Exchange away!

This prayer may sound like this:

> *Lord Jesus, I recognize I've been holding onto fear and have used it to keep me safe. I'm sorry and ask Your forgiveness for doing this. I now choose to break agreement with fear and anxiety and to give up all their protection (which means I will not take fear with me into the car to help me drive more safely, I'm willing to drive again, and I give up the protection of not driving). I command all demonic assignments coming against me because of doing this to go now, in Jesus' name! Lord Jesus, I ask You to please clean out this fear and give me what You value in exchange.*

Be sure to take time to receive from the Lord.

After doing this exchange, check to see how you're feeling about driving now. Do you still feel fearful? If it feels peaceful, then you've gotten a good exchange. If you still feel fear, then go to Chapter 1 to address resistance. If not, determine what you're feeling that's uncomfortable and do another Value Exchange.

In another example, you may be feeling a lot of stress and anxiety at school or work. It feels like this negative energy is helping you work harder and better, getting things done more efficiently. This may be empowered even more from the subconscious belief that if you work hard enough, you won't fail and people won't see you as being not good enough or as a failure. By doing this, you're trying to protect yourself from ever feeling that way again. You might fear that giving up the push from anxiety will cause you to be lazy and not work hard enough. The beliefs "I'm not good enough" and "I'm a failure" are the initial motivators to work harder to protect your heart from being hurt again. Then anxiety comes along to assist by giving you additional motivation.

The problem with using the power of anxiety to protect you from failure and feeling not good enough is that it doesn't STOP pushing you. Therefore, your best efforts will never FEEL "good enough." If you were a train using the power of this negative motivation, it would help you go up the mountain but then the same negative power would push you back down again! It will not let up or slow down and will keep pushing when it's no longer needed, like a train without brakes.

The temptation to use the negative power of anxiety can come from prior experiences in which anxiety felt like it helped you get something done quicker. After completing its task, the feeling of anxiety calms down and remains ready for the next opportunity. Therefore, anxiety is used to alleviate the feeling of anxiety!

Once this cycle of anxiety begins, you might start feeling anxious about things that don't even make sense! You may wake up feeling anxious without any reason.

COPING MECHANISMS ATTACHED TO ANXIETY:

1. **Self-protection/self-motivation:** I do something about a situation, trying to fix it so I can feel safer and in control. In this way, anxiety protects me from feeling out of control.

2. **Self-protection/self-elevation:** I become irritable and angry in response to feeling out of control. Anger makes me feel more powerful and in control.

3. **Self-motivation:** Anxiety helps me work harder and faster in certain situations; when I'm behind at work, anxiety helps me catch up.

4. **Self-justice/self-elevation:** Anxiety causes me to make sure everybody knows I'm a victim of injustice. I resort to gossip and let everybody know how I've been hurt so I can make the offender look bad.

5. **Self-elevation/manipulation and control:** I realize my anxiety has the power to get other people anxious—and I use its power to get people to do what I want.

6. **Self-comfort:** My anxiety causes people to feel sorry for me and cater to my "needs." (I love it when that happens).

7. **Self-comfort:** Anxiety justifies my addiction (e.g., cigarettes, alcohol, drugs), which brings comfort and a feeling of control. This addiction may be the only thing in life I can control. See the Addictions chapter for assistance.

A Value Exchange might be something like this:

Lord Jesus, I recognize I've been using anxiety to motivate myself to work harder to be better so I'm protected from feeling not good enough and a failure. I'm sorry and ask Your forgiveness for doing this. I now choose to break agreement with anxiety and give up all its motivational power and protection. I command all demonic assignments connected to this to go now, in Jesus' name! Lord Jesus, I ask that You please clean this out for me and give to me what You value in exchange.

Be sure to take time to receive from the Lord.

Following the exchange, remember to check for the presence of anxiety or feeling not good enough or failure. Go back into a memory to see if either of those emotions are still present. If so, then you'll need to look for another possible attached coping mechanism and do another Value Exchange.

Another common scenario may be when you become stressed because you have many responsibilities to remember and get done. You may have reminder lists in your mind to help keep track of everything, and you may find yourself replaying the list in your head. This is all very overwhelming, and you start to feel out of control and STRESSED! There is too much to juggle! These emotions can CAUSE you to increase your awareness and push you to think about them even more, maybe trying to reorganize them to feel more in control. In this case, you've partnered with stress and the feeling of being out of control, so you can be more aware and focused on the issues to feel more secure and in control.

A Value Exchange might look like this:

> *Lord Jesus, I've come into agreement with the feeling of being out of control and stressed and have used them to increase my awareness of what is stressing me to help me feel more in control. I ask Your forgiveness for doing this. I now choose to break agreement with using the power of "out of control" and "stressed" and give up all their value. I command all demonic assignments connected to these things to go, in Jesus' name! Lord Jesus, I ask You to clean this place out for me and give me what You value in exchange.*

Be sure to take time to receive from the Lord.

After doing this exchange, check for the feelings of being out of control and stressed. What are you feeling now? Can you feel either one? How do you feel now about the list of responsibilities and tasks?

You will keep in perfect and constant peace the one whose mind is steadfast (that is, committed and focused on You—in both inclination and character), because he trusts and takes refuge in You (with hope and confident expectation).
~*Isaiah 26:3* (AMP)

Prayer:

Jesus, help me in my weakness to come into the revelation of the depths of Your love. I want to KNOW and receive Your love in such a way that I'm empowered to stand in the face of any storm! Bring me into Your secret chambers and teach me Your ways. I want to understand Your heart and the mysteries that surround You. For I desire to be dependent on the strength of Your love for every aspect of my life.

CHAPTER 7

UNFORGIVENESS

Forgiveness can be a tough issue. Many times, we have the desire to forgive and have tried to let the offense(s) go but the feeling still lingers. Other times, we have no desire or intention to forgive at all. Often the situation that needs to be forgiven involves such a deep emotional or physical pain that our heart just does not want to let it go. Forgiving is making a *deliberate choice* to stop feeling upset or resentful toward someone for an offense or event that caused harm or injustice. It also requires cancelling the debt and releasing the person who offended you from "paying you back" what you feel they owe you in return. Forgiveness is NOT condoning the offense, pretending the offense didn't happen, or saying it's okay for others to take advantage of you.

The Greek word used in the Bible for forgive is *aphiemi*, which means to pardon or overlook an offense or debt and treat the offender as not guilty. The offense is "sent away." If a person keeps bringing up the same offense, they never really forgave—and it wasn't really "sent away." In addition to emotional pain, there is often a *feeling of disapproval about the injustice* involved, and the victim often doesn't want to forgive until the person who hurt them takes responsibility for their actions, does something to make amends, or is punished for what they did. Holding onto unforgiveness can progress into other emotions such as anger, resentment, bitterness, hatred, or rage, and it could in some eventually end in thoughts of causing someone else physical harm or, in rare cases, death.

The Bible has much to say about the importance of forgiveness. In Matthew 18:21-35, Jesus talks about the consequence for choosing not to forgive. In this parable, a man was forgiven a very large debt by his lord and was told to act the same forgiving way toward other people who owed him a debt. After getting out of his own debtor's prison, he disobeyed his lord and demanded that another man (owing him a much smaller debt than what was just forgiven him) pay back all the debt owed. When the man couldn't, he insisted the man stay in prison until the entire debt was paid off. Jesus says that the consequence for his actions was the following: "Then the master called the servant in. 'You wicked servant,' he said, 'I canceled all that debt of yours because you begged me to. Shouldn't you have had mercy on your fellow servant just as I had on you?' In anger his master turned him over to the jailers to be tortured, until he should pay back all he owed. This is how my heavenly Father will treat each of you unless you forgive your brother *from the heart*."

We have been completely forgiven because of what Jesus did on the Cross for us, and we need to extend forgiveness to anyone who sins against us. There is a significant consequence when someone refuses to forgive.

> **Whenever you stand praying, if you have anything against anyone, forgive him (drop the issue, let it go), so that your Father who is in heaven will also forgive you your transgressions and wrongdoings (against Him and others). But if you do not forgive, neither will your Father in heaven forgive your transgressions.**
> *~Mark 11:25-26* (AMP)

The first step to being able to forgive would be to identify the specific offense that needs to be "sent away." You could ask yourself, "I am resisting forgiving because they made me feel _____?" Often, our first response is to start putting the focus on the event and what the other person did wrong to you that felt so hurtful or unfair. For example, your mind may keep replaying how rude that was when your colleague from work said something at the staff meeting that made you look bad in front of everybody. Your mind is spinning because it was so embarrassing!

What that person did was so disrespectful! You would never have done that to anybody! Thinking about that rude comment only causes more feelings of pain and anger about the situation. The whole thing wasn't fair! Complete injustice.

To begin to walk through this process of forgiveness, you'll first need to **shift your focus** away from what they did to you and onto how their comment or actions made you feel—and what you believed about yourself because of it. You can only control your own feelings and what you want to do about them. Try not to overthink or overanalyze what happened. That will only make you more frustrated and upset.

How did that make you feel about *yourself?* Write it down on paper. Using the above example, you would have felt shame and believed you were "not good enough" or a failure. You might have felt angry. Write it all down. Be honest with yourself and admit how that felt. If you have problems identifying how you feel, then you can look at the list given in the chapter on Identity Issues. Remember, this is *not* about what the other person did wrong or what they were thinking. It's about how their words or actions *made you feel about yourself.* Don't spend time trying to defend yourself or make sense of anything.

The next time you encounter them, it might be difficult and stressful because of the possibility of being hurt again. The emotional pain becomes attached to the memory of that person, reminding you of what they did to hurt you. By doing this, you'll feel this negative emotion and know what to expect when you are around them. You won't be taken by surprise again. Holding offense against them can also feel like it is pushing them away in self-defense, like a wall of protection. Any heart guard you put up wants to protect you from the possibility of being hurt again. Forgiving may feel like you're putting yourself at risk, causing you to feel unprotected and vulnerable. In this example, NOT forgiving is a type of defense mechanism.

When you experience emotional, physical, or sexual trauma, there is an actual wound created within your soul. That wound is deep and FILLED with gut-wrenching pain. The wound contains these "horrifically" painful emotions along with beliefs about yourself and God, such as feeling "not good enough" or believing that "God doesn't care about me." You may try to ignore, stuff, or bury the pain, not knowing what else to do with it. Forgiveness is not even a possibility because there's no hope of getting rid of the pain or getting justice. Unforgiveness and the coping mechanisms attached to the wound prevent the pain from being released. Because this place of woundedness is still stuck in your soul, that part of your heart is continually being tormented, as Jesus talked about in Matthew 18:21-35.

> RELEASE AND FORGIVE THE PEOPLE WHO HAVE HURT YOU. DOING THIS WILL CREATE A SPACE FOR HIM TO BE THE PROTECTOR OF YOUR HEART.

With sexual abuse, as well as serious physical and/or emotional abuse, there really isn't anything the other person can do that would make up for what has been done. Unconditional forgiveness is the only way to be free from the pain. If you've been the victim of these types of abuse, Jesus has the power to set you free. He WILL bring peace to the memory.

We tend to make forgiveness conditional, putting an expectation on the person who hurt us, demanding they apologize and treat us better. In the example above, your thought process may go something like this: "I will forgive my colleague if ..." and then give conditions that must be met before forgiving him/her. That person would need to apologize and promise to come to you personally if they have issues with your work. You may want them also to publicly apologize because this was an offense against your character. Not forgiving feels justified until your demands are met. Forgiving may feel like it would be sending a message to your colleague that what they did to you was no big deal and please do it again!

Sometimes unforgiveness can feel like it polices and convicts the perpetrators of their hurtful behavior and tries to get them to act better. In doing this, you are actually being controlling and holding their mistake "over their head." Conviction is the job of the Holy Spirit and using unforgiveness to convict them may interfere with God's work in their life. In this place, it's good to let go of control and trust Holy Spirit, who actually has the convicting power to change them, even as He is changing us! We cannot forget that we aren't perfect either. God is working on me too!

By keeping a "chip on your shoulder," and holding onto the grudge or grievance against someone, you're giving that person a lot of power over your emotions and well-being. Your well-being is now dependent on the very person who hurt you! (Isn't that brilliant?) How they treat you on any particular day has become the barometer determining how you feel. Wouldn't it be nice to enjoy every part of your day, even when everyone around you is having a bad day?! You have the free-will power to be able to choose a better way! You do this by giving the responsibility to determine your well-being over to Jesus. His well-being is not determined by what anyone thinks of Him, or by anyone's good or bad mood.

Jesus loves us unconditionally. Our goal should be to learn to love unconditionally in the way our heavenly Father loves us. The Lord once spoke to my own heart saying, "Can you love them if they don't change?" That was very convicting and caused me to pause and consider how to answer that question. Can I? Can I stop holding it against them and send it away? The ultimate act of love was Jesus on the Cross forgiving us, sending away our mistakes and wrongdoings even while being punished and suffering for what we did wrong. Forgiveness is an act of love, and when we forgive, we are walking in love, righteousness, and holiness. Forgiving is acting Christ-like.

> **And this is love: that we walk in accordance with His commandments and are guided continually by His precepts. This is the commandment, just as you have heard from the beginning, that you should (always) walk in love.**
> *~2 John 1:6* (AMP)

Yet, because we live in a fallen world, we will get wounded and need healing for the emotional pain inflicted by other people. The pain feels worse when you're hurt by the people you love or value the most. Unforgiveness doesn't really keep you from being hurt again and puts a wall of division between you and the people you care about. It doesn't really protect you from your enemies either. Only Jesus can effectively do that for you. But first you'll need to release and forgive the people who have hurt you. Doing this will create a space for Him to be the protector of your heart.

People will try to take advantage of you and treat you badly. Jesus will help you make proper boundaries and give you wisdom and strategy to navigate through each trial. Because your heart is protected from their hurtful words and actions, you can create these boundaries in a way that is for their benefit—not just for your own self-protection. You need to stand up against people who are doing wrong, rather than enabling their behavior. It's not good for them to keep walking in selfishness, or controlling or abusive behaviors. With the wisdom of Jesus, you can bring correction in love. If you try to bring correction without first forgiving, it won't be motivated by love and will cause further damage to the relationship.

Unforgiveness can also be a way to bring justice for something that wasn't fair. Often unforgiveness will also cause anger; if so, see the chapter on Anger. Unforgiveness may feel like it's bringing justice because they don't deserve to be forgiven. You may keep them imprisoned in your heart as a way to punish them. They, on the other hand, may not even know you've done it. You feel entitled to keep them there. Keeping them locked up feels like it removes the sting of injustice.

Being wounded is like getting punched in the heart. You will rise up and meet that punch with a countermeasure. You'll wrap a "fist" of unforgiveness around the "fist" of pain. Now these two fists are securely locked together and held in your heart for safekeeping. The person who caused the pain, who you don't even want to think about anymore, is entrapped in your heart and that's all you can think about! Because of this, they will continually have the power to hurt you. The only way to unlock the fist of pain and the fist of unforgiveness is to go before Jesus and forgive.

EXAMPLES OF COPING MECHANISMS RELATED TO UNFORGIVENESS:

1. **Self-protection:** I put up strong boundaries so I can keep the person who hurt me pushed away. Or I might put up a wall so they can't get close to my heart and hurt me again.

2. **Self-protection:** I keep my guard up so I can feel more powerful and less vulnerable around them. Forgiving them may feel like I would be unprotected and open to being hurt again.

3. **Self-protection:** I emotionally disconnect from the person who hurt me so I won't get hurt as badly again. They may not even know I've done this, which makes me feel more in control.

4. **Self-motivation:** Increases the urgency to find creative ways to self-protect. For example, I could find creative excuses to avoid being around someone.

5. **Self-elevation:** Holding unforgiveness (a judgment against them) helps me to feel in control and more powerful because I have the upper hand.

6. **Self-justice:** I try to convict the person who hurt me, making them feel guilty so they'll acknowledge and admit what they did was wrong. This would justify the pain I feel. To forgive would feel like they got away with it without acknowledging their wrongdoing.

7. **Self-justice:** Punishing them in my mind makes me feel better. Getting even feels good, even if it's just in thought!

8. **Self-justice/self-elevation:** I hold what they did "over their head" so they'll feel guilty and try harder to make it up to me because, "I would never have done that to them." Self-comfort: Knowing I am THE victim in this scenario feels comforting. I could use it to get sympathy from others.

For a free printout on "The 5 Ways Coping Mechanism Can Actually Harm You," please visit our website at **FreedomExpress16.org**.

Example 1: Your spouse of 15 years just announced he/she has been having an affair with someone from work for the last year. They do not want a divorce. They want to work things out and expect you to be happy about that. This was such a shock. Initially you don't even know how to think. You're torn between leaving or staying. Both scenarios are difficult to imagine. Either way, you know you need to forgive to be able to move forward, but you're finding it difficult to do so. You're finding it difficult to forgive because you're hurt to the core with feeling betrayed, unloved, disrespected, and worthless. You're using unforgiveness to help you navigate how to make the necessary decisions moving forward. You have also "put up a wall" of protection around your heart so they can't hurt you like that again.

In doing the Value Exchange, it is often helpful to picture yourself putting the person who hurt you onto the altar in front of Jesus.

A Value Exchange for unforgiveness would look like the following:

> *Lord Jesus, I recognize that I've been holding onto unforgiveness and have used it to motivate myself to find ways to protect myself from feeling betrayed, unloved, disrespected, and worthless. I'm using it to make a wall of protection around my heart. I'm sorry and ask Your forgiveness for doing this. I now choose to break agreement with unforgiveness and give up all its ungodly benefits. I command all demonic assignments that have come against me because of this to go, in Jesus' name! Lord Jesus, I ask you to clean this out for me and give to me what You have in exchange.*

Be sure to take time to receive from the Lord.

Remember to check a memory to make sure the unforgiveness and the pain from the connected beliefs are gone.

Example 2: You look back at your life and see the many mistakes and people who you've hurt. You did drugs and disrespected your parents. You had multiple sexual partners. You cheated on your spouse in your first marriage. You drifted away from God for a time and didn't have anything to do with church or Him. The list goes on and on. You're now happily married and feel as though you're doing a pretty good job. But you can't shake the past and you think about it all the time. All these mistakes make you feel like you're "not good enough" and a failure. You now feel conviction and a desire to get right with God, but you don't feel like you are forgiven by God, and certainly not yourself because what you did was "too bad." You could be using unforgiveness to keep yourself in line, making sure you don't do those things again. You could be using it to motivate yourself to try harder to be better. You don't think it would be fair to experience forgiveness because you don't feel like you deserve it, and so you keep yourself punished to make payment for the past. Because there's shame connected with your mistakes, you recognize that keeping yourself guilty and shamed eases the blow when the truth gets exposed and people find out about all the bad things you've done.

A Value Exchange would look like the following:

> *Lord Jesus, I recognize that I've chosen not to forgive myself for being "not good enough" and a failure. I've done this to keep myself in line, motivate myself to try harder, punish myself as a way to take justice, and cushion the blow of people finding out what I've done. I'm sorry and ask Your forgiveness for doing this. Please forgive me. I now choose to forgive myself for all the wrong things I've ever done. I give up unforgiveness and all its ungodly benefits. I command all demonic assignments connected to these things to go, in Jesus' name! Lord Jesus, I ask You to clean this out for me and give me what You have in exchange.*

Be sure to take time to receive from the Lord.

Be sure to go to the chapter on Soul Ties and break all the ungodly soul ties created by having sex outside of marriage. Then check the memories and see if you have forgiven yourself. Do you feel any guilt or shame?

Example 3: A relative sexually abused you as a little child and it continued through your early teens. They strongly impressed upon you that you had to keep this a secret, and you believed them. You believed you were keeping your family safe by not telling. The abuse made you feel dirty, worthless, and shameful and that "it was my fault" and "I must have done something to make them do that." Try as you might to get past the feelings, you can't seem to stop playing the scenario in your head all the time. When you see the person, you have great fear. The unforgiveness motivates you to avoid situations where you must be around the perpetrator. It also taught you not to trust anybody or let anybody too close in an intimate way.

A Value Exchange would look like the following:

> *Lord Jesus, I recognize that I've been holding onto unforgiveness toward the person who abused me because they made me feel dirty, worthless, and shameful, and that it was my fault. I've used unforgiveness and the fear I've attached to it to motivate me to self-protect by putting up walls and avoiding situations when I'm around them. I now choose to break agreement with unforgiveness and to give up all its ungodly value. I command all demonic assignments to go now, in Jesus' name! Lord Jesus, I ask You to clean this out and give to me what You value in exchange.*

Be sure to take time to receive from the Lord.

After making this exchange, go to the chapter on Soul Ties and break the ungodly soul tie created against you. Then check and see how you feel about that person now. Do you still feel unforgiveness? Then check the memory(s) for the remaining feelings addressed above (fear, shame, worthless, it's your fault, you're dirty.) Check for these feelings one at a time. If the memory is peaceful, you have gotten a good exchange! If not, then address any remaining negative feelings and any feelings of resistance.

Prayer:

Papa, sometimes I'm at a loss for words. Your intentional, persistent, and faithful love brings me to my knees! Jesus, oh precious Jesus, "thank you" seems like such a small effort in my desire to express my gratitude to you. For it is because You willingly allowed Yourself to become death for me so that I can be made righteous in Papa's eyes! Oh, what joy!!! And now because I've been made righteous, I am now carrying within me the very presence of Your Holy Spirit. Holy Spirit, help me to be ever conscious of You. Help me to remember that with You, I have all I need to be victorious in every trial and can truly run this race as if to win!!! Oh, how I love You!

CHAPTER 8

GUILT

Everyone makes mistakes. Nobody gets it all perfect.

Guilt is a feeling of worry or unhappiness that can come from knowing you have done something wrong. You might feel guilty when you hurt someone you love. It's connected with a feeling of shame that can be felt down into the deepest places of your soul and can even be physically nauseating. If not dealt with, guilt can cause you to start condemning and even hating yourself.

Guilt can come from an actual list of offenses or crimes you have committed, but it can also be a false perception, without actual proof you have done something wrong. Guilt can also be something another person wants you to feel, although you haven't even done anything wrong (from your viewpoint). Sometimes people want to give you a "guilt trip" to get what they want and to control you. Other times, they might punish you to feel better by delivering their own justice. They may "hold over your head" those mistakes to remind you not to mess up again.

Other times, we are freely forgiven by others and cannot seem to forgive ourselves. Sometimes we feel like our mistake was just "too big" and "too horrible" for Jesus to forgive and that we don't deserve His forgiveness.

Whatever the reason, guilt is toxic and needs to be dealt with in a healthy way. The salvation message is that Jesus Christ came as a man and chose to pay the consequence for our sins so that we can be forgiven.

> **Therefore there is now no condemnation for those who are in Christ Jesus.**
> ~*Romans 8:1* *(NASB)*

> **He cancelled out every legal document we had on our record and the old arrest warrant that stood to indict us. He erased it all—our sins, our stained soul—He deleted it all and they cannot be retrieved! Everything we once were in Adam has been placed on the cross and nailed permanently there as a public display of cancellation.**
> ~*Colossians 2:14* *(TPT)*

We are all guilty before God. The Bible states, "For all have sinned and fall short of the glory of God" (Romans 3:23). If you have sinned, then you're convicted and declared guilty of a criminal offense against God. When you feel that conviction, you have the opportunity to repent and ask for forgiveness. Too often we do not even think or remember to ask for forgiveness. You may have grown up believing that Jesus paid the price for your forgiveness, and you might ask, "Why should I ask God for forgiveness again? My sins are forgiven."

> **Therefore, confess your sins to one another (your false steps, your offenses), and pray for one another, that you may be healed and restored. The heartfelt and persistent prayer of a righteous man (believer) can accomplish much (when put into action and made effective by God—it is dynamic and can have tremendous power).**
> ~*James 5:16* *(AMP)*

On the contrary, you may not be able to think of any sins you've committed. However, we aren't always aware of our sins of omission (what we should have done and did not do).

This is a good place to ask yourself,
"Are there any sins I've committed that I need to ask God/Jesus to forgive?"

Holy Spirit brings conviction that makes us aware of our guilt with the intention of bringing us to repentance. He does not hold you in condemnation. If you're still feeling condemnation after asking for forgiveness, then you're either feeling your sin is too bad to forgive or you cannot forgive yourself for some reason. As hard as this may seem, if you struggle with guilt *and* you're a Christian, then you are CHOOSING to keep feeling that way. Guilt will CAUSE you to find ways to cope.

EXAMPLES OF COPING MECHANISMS RELATED TO GUILT:

1. **Self-protection/self-justice:** I punish myself to take justice. Taking justice makes me feel better.

2. **Self-motivation:** I work harder to be better.

3. **Self-motivation:** I give up even trying to be better. "What's the point?"

4. **Self-protection:** I put up a wall of protection by numbing my heart to keep others from hurting me so much.

5. **Self-protection/self-elevation:** I rise up in anger, yelling at them to protect myself, to fight back, and to regain control.

6. **Self-protection:** I do whatever they want me to do so they won't get upset with me. Saying no to their requests would make me feel bad about myself.

7. **Self-protection:** Since I feel guilty around a certain person, I know what treatment to expect from them. As a result, their actions and words don't hurt so bad because I agree with them. In this way, I protect my heart from feeling worse.

8. **Self-elevation**: I do nice things for the person I hurt so they'll appreciate me more and hopefully treat me with more respect. In this way, I'm trying to manipulate how they treat me.

9. **Self-comfort:** Feeling sorry for myself feels good and might draw comfort from others (self-pity).

Example 1: A mother feels guilty because she believes she didn't do a good enough job raising her children. She sees them struggling with life and feels like it's her fault for not being there enough while they were growing up. She believes she should have stayed home more. She should have helped them more with schoolwork. She should have taught them more about God and maybe they would have made better choices. The list goes on and on. She continues to live in regret and *perceived* guilt (she may or may not even be guilty of what she's believing). She can't go back and change the past, even if she did make a mistake. Therefore, she may cope with this by punishing herself. Keeping herself punished makes her feel better about the situation because she's doing to herself what she feels she deserves. *She is using punishment to bring her own justice.* Bringing justice in this way takes away the sting of guilt. She has used the guilt to protect her heart from feeling *as guilty* because she is being punished. The benefits of doing this are self-justice and self-protection.

Her Value Exchange would be as follows:

Prayer:

Lord Jesus, I recognize that I've been holding onto guilt and have used it to bring my own justice by keeping myself punished and to hopefully feel less guilty. I ask Your forgiveness for doing this. I now choose to break agreement with guilt and to give up all its protection and justice. I command all demonic assignments that have come against me because of this to go now, in Jesus' name! Lord Jesus, I ask that You clean this place out for me and give me what You value in exchange.

Be sure to take time to receive from the Lord.

In the example on the previous page, the mother may also choose to use guilt in a way that motivates her to be a better mother to her children by causing her to try harder. In this example, guilt is being used to "police" herself so she won't make the same mistakes again.

The Value Exchange would be as follows:

> *Lord Jesus, I recognize that I've been holding onto guilt and have used it to motivate me to be a better mother and to keep me from making mistakes. I ask Your forgiveness for doing this. I now choose to break agreement with guilt and to give up all its motivation. I command all demonic assignments that have come against me because of this to go now, in Jesus' name! Lord Jesus, I ask that You clean this place out for me and give me what You value in exchange.*

Be sure to take time to receive from the Lord.

The same mother may someday find out that her children are blaming her for their current problems. This actually happens. They believe the failures in their lives are her fault. Sometimes this is intentional, to "lay a guilt trip" on their mother to manipulate her into making amends and to get what they want from her. They may actually believe they're not doing anything wrong. They may blame her to get revenge or to make her a scapegoat, so they're not responsible or held accountable for their own actions. Regardless of the reason, she may find herself feeling guilty and just cannot shake it.

She may want to make it up to them and finds herself taking on responsibilities for her children that they should be doing themselves. She also might try to protect them from getting into trouble by taking the blame for what they've done wrong. Doing these things for them makes her feel like she's being a good mom and will elevate her standing in their eyes. They may so frequently blame and shame her for their failures that she'll start to believe it, even when she previously knew she wasn't a failure. She may subconsciously put a *guard* around her heart to prepare herself for the next assault.

At this point, the mother is being completely controlled by her children. This has created an ungodly soul tie with her children that needs to be broken. At some level, this developed as a coping mechanism to guard her heart. The next step would be to go to the Soul Ties chapter.

Example 2: Another possible situation that might bring guilt and shame is when you're caught doing ungodly things. For some reason, doing something wrong doesn't always feel bad until you're caught. Examples may include pornography, addiction to drugs or alcohol, lying, adultery, stealing, gossip, having an abortion, and other things that cause destruction and pain to other people and yourself. This would also put a wedge between you and God. Being exposed for doing these things is so humiliating and shameful it can be very difficult to forgive yourself. Because it's just *so bad.* "It's not even forgivable!"

For example, let's say your involvement with pornography was discovered by your spouse. However, you rationalized this in your own mind and really don't think it's wrong. You don't understand why your spouse would be so upset. But you do recognize that when people find out, they'll judge you and look down on you for doing it. The humiliation of being caught would cause great guilt and shame *because of what other people would think of you now if they find out.* This loss of respect could be your biggest fear. Fear wants to get you ready for the shame, softening the blow. The fear of losing respect will keep you from admitting your sin. Addressing this fear exposes the sin.

The prayer for this would look like:

Prayer:

Lord Jesus, I recognize I've used fear of what other people think about me to protect my heart from feeling shame and disrespect. I've used it to motivate me to act in a way that would cause others to think the best of me. I ask forgiveness for doing this. I choose to break agreement with fear and its ungodly benefits of motivation and protection. I command all ungodly assignments connected to these things to go, in Jesus' name. Lord Jesus, I ask that You clean this place out and give me what You value in exchange.

Be sure that you take time to receive from the Lord.

Hopefully now that you've addressed the fear, you should be able to address the sin. The Lord's heart is that we each would humble ourselves, recognize our own sin, and repent. After asking for forgiveness, you may still feel guilt and shame. By holding onto guilt and shame, you might use it to motivate yourself to find ways to keep from doing it again. Also, not forgiving yourself would allow guilt and shame to keep you punished. Because you don't feel that you deserve God's forgiveness, you bring your own justice.

When we don't feel like we deserve it, it's true. There's nothing we can do to earn forgiveness. We don't deserve a single Value Exchange—not even the ones *not* related to guilt! But at some point, we need to accept the reality of the amazing grace and mercy of God.

Would you be willing to allow Jesus to share His heart with you and give you His perspective concerning the belief that *you need to hold onto the guilt and shame to punish yourself*? If so, just invite Him to do that right now. After doing this, does it feel okay to move forward with forgiving yourself?

Prayer:

Lord Jesus, I recognize I've sinned by indulging in pornography and I ask Your forgiveness for doing this. And I choose to receive Your forgiveness and I choose to forgive myself. I recognize I've used guilt and shame for self-motivation and self-justice by keeping myself punished. And I've used pornography to self-comfort and self-elevate. I ask forgiveness for all these things. I command all ungodly assignments connected to all these things to go now, in Jesus' name! Lord Jesus, I ask You to clean this place out and give me what You value in exchange.

Be sure that you take time to receive from the Lord.

After doing this exchange, does it still feel true that you need to feel guilty? If not, then you've gotten an exchange! If this still feels true, go to the section in Chapter 1 on Dealing With Resistance.

After doing the Exchange, you will need to refer to the chapter on Closing the Gates. If the pornography has become an addiction, see the Addictions chapter.

In Him we have redemption (that is, our deliverance and salvation) through His blood, (which paid the penalty for our sin and resulted in) the forgiveness and complete pardon of our sin, in accordance with the riches of His grace.
~Ephesians 1:7 (AMP)

Prayer:

Oh Lord, set my heart on fire! Pull me into a place where I trust Your love and allow it to touch me deep in the most secret chambers of my heart. Draw me to You in a way that I can surrender everything to You that hinders love. Help me feel Your love and be able to love You with my whole self. Amen.

WOULD YOU BE WILLING TO ALLOW JESUS TO SHARE HIS HEART WITH YOU AND GIVE YOU HIS PERSPECTIVE CONCERNING THE BELIEF THAT *YOU NEED TO HOLD ONTO THE GUILT AND SHAME TO PUNISH YOURSELF?*

CHAPTER 9

ANGER/SELF-ANGER

nger is an intense emotion of annoyance, displeasure, or hostility, typically occurring in response to feeling hurt, offended, or threatened. In this way, there's always something hiding behind the anger. Under its influence, you might lose self-control and it could affect your ability to discern the situation correctly. Anger is an emotion we all feel at some time or another. Some common phrases used in a moment of anger include: *makes my blood boil, ruffles my feathers, gets under my skin, makes me see red, pisses me off, pushes my buttons*, and *makes me want to explode.* The common theme in all these statements are the words "me" or "my." Unrighteous anger revolves around ME!

The Bible says we will get angry, but not to sin in our anger. What makes it sin?

> **Be angry (at sin—at immorality, at injustice, at ungodly behavior), yet do not sin; do not let your anger (cause you shame, nor allow it to) last until the sun goes down. And do not give the devil an opportunity (to lead you into sin by holding a grudge, or nurturing anger, or harboring resentment, or cultivating bitterness).**
> *~Ephesians 4:26-27* (AMP)

From the Scripture on the previous page, we see that anger is to be momentary and not last until sundown. Additionally, anger leading to sin will cause you to act shamefully and you'll harbor it by holding a grudge, unforgiveness, resentment, and/or bitterness. Feeding anger will cause it to grow. Like an infection, it will multiply and progress. When fully expressed, it turns into retaliation, wrath, hatred, violence, and even murderous thoughts and actions.

> **Let everyone be quick to hear (be a careful, thoughtful**
> **listener), slow to speak (a speaker of carefully chosen**
> **words and) slow to anger (patient, reflective, forgiving);**
> **for the (resentful, deep-seated) anger of man does not**
> **produce the righteousness of God (that standard of**
> **behavior which He requires from us).**
> *~James 1:19-20* (AMP)

Unfortunately, because of our woundedness, most people struggle with anger that is unrighteous. It is important to recognize whether your anger is righteous or unrighteous. Righteous anger is "legal" in God's Kingdom, whereas unrighteous anger is sinful, or "illegal." Righteous anger is God-centered and focused on the Kingdom and the issues God is concerned about. Unrighteous anger is self-focused and centered upon your own rights and concerns.

RIGHTEOUS ANGER	UNRIGHTEOUS ANGER
Legal	Illegal
God-centered	Me-centered
Kingdom-focused	Me-focused

To know the difference between these types of anger, you'll need to evaluate your **MOTIVE, ATTITUDE, and ACTIONS.**

1. MOTIVE:

First, you'll need to ask yourself why you're angry.

Anger arises in response to how some person/people or situation made you feel. Anger is always a response to another emotion or belief. Ask yourself, "I am angry because I feel *what?*" _____ (Fill in the blank.)

Unrighteous anger occurs when you take someone's behavior or a situation personally and are motivated to respond for that reason. How does the situation make you feel about *your* rights and concerns? Were you offended? Why? Don't focus on what the other person did wrong or try to rationalize their actions. What was done to you and why it was done needs to be "put on a shelf" so you can focus on *how it made you feel.* For example, you might be angry because someone was rude and made you feel worthless, stupid, or incompetent. Anger is being motivated by those feelings.

> It is important to recognize whether your anger is righteous or unrighteous. Righteous anger is "legal" in God's Kingdom, whereas unrighteous anger is sinful, or "illegal."

Becoming angry when someone hurts you is an automatic subconscious reaction that happens reflexively in self-defense. In this way, anger is a *"secondary" emotion*, meaning it is triggered by another negative emotion. You need to find out what emotion or belief triggered the anger. In the example above, feeling worthless was a trigger.

Righteous anger will be motivated by what is offensive to God. This type of anger is *legal* because it is *God-centered* and focused on *His Kingdom* and *His concerns.* Examples of what angers God include unjust treatment of others (child abuse, pornography, sex-trafficking, racism, abortion, adultery, gossip), worshiping idols (like money, popular people, jobs), unbelief, and refusal to repent. God's anger is directed at evil and is motivated by what is just, loving, and righteous. He loves justice, and His commandments to love God and love each other are motivated by His love for humanity. Righteous anger is legal because it is directed toward the injustice and wrong treatment of other people.

2. ATTITUDE:

The second question to ask is, "What is my attitude?"

Attitude is a way of thinking or feeling about someone or something. How are you feeling about that person you're angry with?

An unrighteous attitude is smug, proud, and condescending and wants to put the person who hurt you "in their place." This attitude judges people by looking down on them—often with contempt—and attaches a negative, demeaning label or value on them. This prideful, self-righteous attitude is similar to how the Pharisees (that Jesus encountered) viewed other people. This *does not accomplish the righteousness of God* and clearly does not reflect His loving character. Our perfect and Holy Lord was treated horribly, disrespected, and abused but did not respond in anger. In experiencing the worst injustice of all eternity, His death on the Cross, He was still able to say, "Father, forgive them; for they do not know what they are doing (Luke 23:34)."

A righteous attitude will come from being in *alignment* with God's perspective of people or situations. Righteous indignation will cause you to feel appalled about the injustice and you'll want to take some action to make things right. This type of anger will seek to find a way to help without harboring bad feelings toward the one who caused the injustice. For example, if someone at work was blatantly disrespectful to you in front of your peers, *righteous anger* would recognize this behavior is wrong, but your *attitude* might be one of compassion toward them because you realize they're acting out of their own wounded thinking. You would be able to respond to them in a way that's not intentionally disrespectful in return.

> **Never repay evil for evil.**
> **Do not be overcome and conquered by evil,**
> **but overcome evil with good.**
> *~Romans 12:17, 21* (AMP)

3. ACTIONS:

The third question to ask when you are angry is, "What are my actions?" or "How does this situation make me want to respond or act in return?"

With unrighteous anger, you lose your temper, your peace, and often feel out of control with your emotions. Are you wanting to curse? Punch them? Spit on them? Push them? Or do you find yourself getting louder, yelling, screaming, or going into a full meltdown of rage? Do you want to avoid them or give them the silent treatment? Do you just want to throw a temper tantrum ("because I can")? Break or throw something? Do you want to get revenge by slandering them and shaming them in front of others? Is this causing you to spiral into self-pity or despair? These are all examples of unrighteous actions.

Righteous anger will be consistent with God's holiness and loving character. His anger is always under control and He does not "lose His temper." Does your behavior reflect God and the life of Christ? Righteous anger will stir you up without losing your peace. You'll be able to respond to injustice with constructive correction and self-control. From the example on the previous page, when you were disrespected at work, the righteous anger might cause you to calmly take your co-worker aside and talk to them about how that made you feel. You may ask them to come to you privately in the future if they have concerns about your work.

> **Treat others the same way you want them to treat you.**
> **But love (that is, unselfishly seek the best or higher good for)**
> **your enemies, and do good, and lend, expecting nothing in**
> **return; for your reward will be great (rich, abundant), and you**
> **will be sons of the Most High; because He Himself is kind and**
> **gracious and good to the ungrateful and the wicked.**
> *~Luke 6:31, 35* (AMP)

There's a big difference between judging a person and judging their behavior. Judging a person causes you to place less value on them. Judging a situation or a person's actions as either right or wrong is desirable and recommended. God instituted a standard of conduct He considers as righteous, and standards of conduct He considers to be wrong. From the beginning, He warned that blessings come with obedience and curses come from disobedience to His standard.

> **Let all bitterness and wrath and anger and clamor**
> **(perpetual animosity, resentment, strife, fault-finding**
> **and slander be put away from you, along with every kind**
> **of malice (all spitefulness, verbal abuse, malevolence).**
> **Be kind and helpful to one another, tender-hearted**
> **(compassionate, understanding), forgiving once another**
> **(readily and freely), just as God in Christ also forgave you.**
> *~Ephesians 4:31-32* (AMP)

SOME POSSIBLE COPING MECHANISMS ATTACHED TO ANGER ARE:

1. **Self-protection/elevation**: I raise my voice to keep someone from taking advantage of me, by intimidating them so I can get my way.

2. **Self-protection/elevation**: In situations where I feel powerless, anger helps me regain control and power, protecting myself from being overpowered. For example, I can use anger against someone who is verbally or physically abusive toward me to defend myself and get them to back off.

3. **Self-protection**: Even if not overtly expressed, being angry with someone can *feel* like it keeps them pushed away from me. This may feel like it will keep them from hurting me again.

4. **Self-motivation**: Channeling the negative power of anger helps to accomplish more by empowering me to work more efficiently, faster, or harder.

5. **Self-elevation**: Anger makes me feel above and more powerful than other people. By using it, I exert control over other people.

6. **Self-elevation**: Anger will give me a voice when I feel I'm not being heard, acknowledged, or being taken seriously. I can force them to listen to me.

7. **Self-justice:** I can punish someone who hurt me and bring justice by using anger, "because they deserve it." (Sometimes they don't even know I'm angry; staying angry with them in my mind feels like it is bringing justice).

8. **Self-comfort:** Anger give me a euphoric feeling or "a release" from built-up tension or anxiety. It's also comforting that I've done something to protect myself (there is great satisfaction in revenge)!

9. **Self-comfort:** Anger feels better than feeling sad.

10. **Self-justice:** "I have a right to be angry and I will find a way to do something about it!"

Value Exchange Examples:

Example 1. You find it difficult to deal with frustrations in life. You're easily upset when the car in front of you is driving too slowly so you act out by honking your horn and tailgating them. You leave restaurants in anger when the waitress doesn't come to your table soon enough. When working on a project that's not going well, you get angry, throw your tools onto the ground, and snap at your kids or coworkers when they ask what's wrong. Even the sound of someone chewing "loudly" is annoying, and you tersely ask them to stop.

What are the values of anger in this example?

1. In the car example, *you're angry because you feel out of control.* You use anger to try to get control by trying to force the other driver to go faster. Anger may be used to intimidate and scare the other driver into submission.

2. At the restaurant, *you're angry because you feel disrespected* and use anger to take justice by showing contempt toward the waitress and business.

3. While doing the project, *you're angry because you felt out of control* when it wasn't going well. Throwing tools gives you a momentary "release." Snapping at someone will let them know you're angry so they will either get out of your way or do something to help you.

4. *You're angry because you feel out of control* when someone won't chew their food quietly and so responding tersely to them will get them to stop.

A Value Exchange may sound like this:

Lord Jesus, I recognize I've used anger to help me feel in control in situations where I feel frustrated and out of control. I have also used anger to control other people and to take justice for being disrespected. Anger has motivated my actions. I'm sorry and ask Your forgiveness for doing this. I now choose to break agreement with anger and to give up its value. I command all demonic assignments connected to this to go, in Jesus' name! Lord Jesus, I ask You to clean this out for me and give to me what You value in exchange.

Take time to receive from the Lord.

After saying this prayer, put yourself back into the memories of those situations and see if you still feel any of the emotions of frustration, out of control, disrespected, or angry.

Example 2: Another situation might be in an office setting in which you're constantly being taken advantage of. The other side of the office has favor with the boss and always gets extra help while you struggle to catch up. You have requested help on many occasions, only to get the shaft again! You are quick to help other people get their work done by the end of the day, but they don't offer to help you. This causes you to be angry, make snide comments, and talk to other people about them. You frequently threaten, "I'm so done with this!"

What are the values of anger in this example?

You're angry because you feel disrespected, powerless, and "it's not fair" (injustice).

1. Anger rises up to protect, to give you power, and to take justice.

2. Anger helps to cover up the sting of disrespect in your heart.

3. You hold a grudge against the people involved and talk about them because it feels justified and gives you a sense of taking justice, making the "wrong right."

4. Talking negatively about them to co-workers makes you feel better about yourself, especially when they agree you're being mistreated.

5. The comment spoken in anger, "I'm so done with this" may give you a sense of control when you're feeling out of control to change anything.

A Value Exchange may sound like this:

Lord Jesus, I recognize I've used anger for protection, control, to feel better about myself, to take justice, and to comfort my heart when I feel hurt and taken advantage of. I've used the phrase, "I'm so done with this" in anger to feel more in control. I ask Your forgiveness for doing this. I now choose to break agreement with anger and to give up all its value. I command all demonic assignments that have come against me because of this to go, in Jesus' name! Lord Jesus, I ask that You clean this out for me and give to me what You value in exchange.

Be sure to take time to receive from the Lord.

After doing this exchange, check the memory to see if you still feel any anger. Also check for the feelings of disrespect, powerlessness, and injustice.

Example 3: As a child, you experienced a parent's anger toward you AND saw how they used anger with your siblings and other people. Initially this made you feel "not good enough" and "I can never get it right." You tried as hard as you could to be perfect, without success. Eventually you realized that retaliating in anger felt more powerful than withdrawing in hurt and fear. As a teenager, you tried to assert your voice in the house and combat anger with anger. As time went on, yelling in your house just seemed like a normal way to communicate feelings. Later in life, you meet someone and fall in love. You recognize they're hurt by your anger. When you have children, you find yourself hurting them as well. You decide you would like to break this generational agreement with anger but don't know how to do it.

How are you benefiting from anger in the above example?

As a child you're angry because you feel "not good enough," "I'll never get it right," "I have no voice," and "I feel powerless."

1. *You're angry at yourself because you believe that "I'm not good enough" and "I'll never get it right."* This self-anger initially <u>motivates</u> you to try harder to be better.

2. *You're angry because you feel powerless* and the anger feels powerful.

3. *You're angry because you feel like you have no voice.* Anger gives you a voice, forcing people listen to you.

4. *You're angry at the injustice toward you* and you have the right to be and stay angry at them until you see justice served.

In this case, the anger is generational because you learned from your parents that using anger gets results.

A Value Exchange might look like this:

Lord Jesus, I recognize I've taken on a generational agreement with anger. I've used this to self-protect, self-motivate, self-comfort, to bring justice, and to make sure my voice is heard. I'm sorry and ask Your forgiveness for doing this. I also choose to forgive my ancestors for bringing this on. I now choose to break agreement with this generational anger and give up all its benefits. I command all demonic assignments that have come against me because of this to go, in Jesus' name! Lord Jesus, I ask You to clean this out for me and please give me what You have in exchange.

Take time to receive from the Lord.

Remember to check a recent memory to see if you still feel angry, powerless, or without a voice. Check a childhood memory as well. It's possible to have other emotions and beliefs in those childhood memories that will need to be dealt with next. If so, identify them and prepare for another Value Exchange.

SELF-ANGER

Sometimes anger is directed at *yourself* instead of toward other people, objects, or situations. In doing this, you are "pointing your finger" at yourself, looking at your faults and what's wrong with you. Multiple negative emotions can be self-directed such as unforgiveness, anger, resentment, bitterness, and even self-hatred. If you're doing this, ask yourself, "What am I believing about myself that would cause me to direct these negative emotions toward me?" Self-directed anger is a way to help cope with these negative self-beliefs. Other coping mechanisms can be found in the Identity chapter in this manual. Using self-anger to cope replaces the help available from the Holy Spirit.

Some possible values of self-anger are listed below:

1. **Self-protection**: By directing anger toward myself, I won't be hurt as badly when someone else doesn't approve of me or gets angry with me.

2. **Self-motivation/self-protection**: Using self-anger, I can police myself and make sure I don't do something that will cause me to feel hurt again. "You're stupid! Why did you do that!!!?"

3. **Self-motivation/self-comfort**: I can physically hit myself or use other methods to self-harm as a way to release the anger I'm feeling against myself. (A child who has experienced physical abuse by an angry person would have observed how the abuser calmed down after the beating. In that way, this behavior is learned by association. Beating myself releases the anger and brings calmness).

4. **Self-justice**: I punish myself with anger to take justice for something I did wrong. "I deserve it." Taking justice feels good!

5. **Self-comfort**: Being angry with myself draws attention from others, who then comfort me, trying to convince me of my good qualities.

Example of self-anger:

Example 1: As a child, your parents were always angry and didn't compliment or encourage you in your efforts to please them. You begin to think everything you do is wrong and "not good enough." Growing up, you might think, "There I go again," finding fault with yourself and unable to see the good. You feel like a failure. As an adult, you can't stop being hard on yourself.

To find the value of self-anger in this example, ask yourself this question, "I'm angry because I feel *what*?" _____
(Fill in the blank.)

You're angry with yourself because you feel like a failure and not good enough.

Some possible values of self-anger are listed below:

1. You're being hard on yourself and using self-anger to motivate you to try harder to be better.
2. Your statement "There I go again" will cushion the disappointment of getting it wrong again and feeling not good enough.

A Value Exchange might look like this:

Lord Jesus, I recognize I've agreed with the belief that I'm not good enough and that I'm a failure. And I've used self-anger to motivate me to try harder to be better and to protect me from those beliefs. I ask forgiveness for holding onto these things and I choose to break agreement with the belief that I'm not good enough and a failure and the way I've used self-anger for motivation and protection. I command all demonic assignments connected to these things to go now, in Jesus' name! I ask You to clean this out for me and give to me what You value in exchange.

Take time to receive from the Lord.

Remember to check a memory where you know you would feel those emotions and see how it feels now. Does it still feel true that you're a failure and not good enough? Are you still directing anger toward yourself? If it feels peaceful, then you have gotten a good exchange! If it isn't peaceful, then identify and address any remaining negative emotions.

Example 2: While in high school, you had your first serious relationship and were intimate, going against your religious beliefs. Shortly after that, the relationship broke up because they no longer respected you. Now you feel the sting of feeling rejected and worthless (like a piece of trash). You also feel guilty (shame) and like a failure for having sex. These feelings cause you to be constantly angry with yourself for making wrong choices. You find yourself saying, in condemnation, "Why do you have to be so stupid! You can't do anything right!" You scold and shame yourself repeatedly.

You're angry with yourself because you made a bad choice that caused you to feel worthless, rejected, like a failure, shamed, and guilty.

Some possible values for self-anger are listed below:

1. You're using anger (rather than relying on the Lord) to motivate yourself to act better and to avoid making that mistake again.

2. You're using anger to help you make better choices in order to protect yourself from feeling worthless, rejected, and shamed again.

3. You could be angry toward yourself because you feel so strongly that you deserve it for going against your morals. Anger is a way to bring justice by self-punishment.

A Value Exchange might look like this:

Lord Jesus, I recognize that I've directed anger toward myself as a way to motivate me to not make the same mistake again. Doing this also protects me from feeling shame, worthless, and like a failure. I have used self-anger and condemnation to punish myself as a way to take justice. I ask Your forgiveness for doing this. I now choose to break agreement with self-anger and condemnation and give up all the value attached to it. I command that all demonic assignments connected to these things have to go now, in Jesus' name! Lord Jesus, I ask You to clean this out for me and give me what You have in exchange.

Take time to receive from the Lord.

Remember to check a memory to see if ALL the emotions listed above are gone. Is the memory peaceful? Do you still have that inner voice of condemnation? What are you hearing now? If there are any negative emotions, identify what is present and address them with a Value Exchange.

> **… since all have sinned and continually fall short of the glory of God, and are being justified (declared free of the guilt of sin, made acceptable to God, and granted eternal life) as a gift by His (precious, undeserved) grace, through the redemption (the payment for our sin) which is (provided) in Christ Jesus …**
> *~Romans 3:23-24* [(AMP)]

Example 3: In your youth, you became sickly with asthma and then developed allergies. Your health continued to deteriorate, and you developed arthritis at a young age, along with skin issues, irritable bowel syndrome, hypothyroidism, and eventually fibromyalgia. Nothing you did made any difference. Prayer. Diets. Medicines. Doctor recommendations. Nothing changed. Your body isn't cooperating with anything you try. Then you even get diagnosed with cancer! Each of these diseases becomes evidence of your body betraying you. With each additional illness, you become angered, feeling betrayed and let down by your own body.

You're angry with your body because you feel frustrated, out of control, like a failure, and hopeless.

Some possible values for self-anger are listed below:

You could motivate yourself to try harder to find a way to help yourself feel better.

1. Using anger, you push your body in unhealthy ways, such as not resting when you should or pushing yourself to work too hard. "I will beat my body into submission."

2. Because you are blaming yourself for having the health problems, you direct anger toward yourself. This anger could motivate you to entertain thoughts of suicide as a way to escape the pain.

3. You could physically abuse your body (even by hitting, burning, or cutting yourself) because your body deserves to be punished. In doing this, you're using the anger to bring justice.

4. By directing anger toward your body (which has failed you), you will not have to take the blame for your failures. "This is my body's fault, not mine."

A Value Exchange might look like this:

Lord Jesus, I recognize I'm holding anger toward myself and my body. I have used this anger to motivate me to try harder to find a solution so I can feel more in control and hopeful. I've also used anger to feel less like a failure by blaming my body. I've punished my body as a way to bring correction by giving it what it deserves (self-justice). I ask Your forgiveness for doing these things. I choose to break agreement with self-anger and all the values I have placed on it. I command all demonic assignments connected to all these things to go now, in Jesus' name! Lord Jesus, please clean this out for me and give me what You have in exchange.

Take time to receive from the Lord.

Remember to check and see if you can still tap into the self-anger. How do you feel about your body now? Do you still feel frustrated, out of control, hopeless, or like a failure? If any of those still feel true, take that specific feeling and do another Value Exchange. It's possible that there is a benefit you missed.

Prayer:

You, oh Lord, are a God of extremes! You are so amazing. Your character leaves me speechless. I have trouble wrapping my mind around the deep things that make up who You are. Alpha and Omega—the beginning and the end. You know no limits to power—You are ALL powerful! All knowledge and wisdom originate from You. You are absolute perfection ... without sin ... Holy ... righteous ... Your justice is without flaw. Even in Your love, You are extreme for You are love in its purest form. You are the expression of extreme grace, mercy, and compassion. The one that leaves me completely undone is Your extreme humility. These extreme attributes caused You to lay it all down—Your divine supernatural identity—and take on a human form like mine. With joy beyond my comprehension, You endured the humiliation of paying for my sin on the Cross. Oh God, how is that possible? It is only because You are a God of extremes and I so love You for that.

CHAPTER 10

PRIDE AND FALSE HUMILITY

PRIDE

Pride is a self-elevating emotional response or a self-important attitude based upon things like education, accomplishments, abilities, physical appearance, and who you know. Pride is self-exalting and takes credit for these accomplishments rather than being thankful and giving credit to God. The world doesn't see anything wrong with pride, viewing it as a positive quality. Much of the world has bought into humanism—a belief that leaves God and the supernatural realm out, denying their existence. As a result, man alone is given credit for every good thing. Therefore, human effort alone is needed to meet the needs in this world. This contrasts with humility, which recognizes God as being the Source of life and all good things.

Pride causes you to compare yourself with others and "look down" on them because of your own wounded emotions. By looking for people you consider to be "less than me," you feel better about yourself. For example, you might look down on anyone who hasn't achieved the level of education, athletic accomplishment(s), wealth, or physical appearance you have. You might also look for people whom you consider to be an "equal" or "higher" status, searching for ways to put them down so you feel better. In doing these comparisons, you're searching for your "place" or significance.

In this way, pride can be "motherly," wanting to take care of you. Pride wants to get you what you deserve and attempts to cover up negative feelings about yourself so you don't feel them.

You may also respond in pride when you feel belittled, "put down," or attacked. For example, if you perceive someone is treating you like you're stupid, or they outright criticize you to your face, your automatic reflex will be to get angry, looking at them critically in response. Pride wants to help you "put them down" or "put them in their place." This feels good because it "equalizes" the playing field and takes justice. Anytime you don't feel valued, pride is like a mother hen, wanting to "talk you up," so you feel better about yourself.

Sometimes pride is motivated by self-importance and superiority. This isn't coming from a low self-image and woundedness, but occurs in someone who feels confident, capable, and has a high self-image. These people are successful, have power, know it, and expect you to treat them accordingly. The world does revolve around them (or so they think)! This is narcissistic thinking and arrogant.

C.S. Lewis states, "As long as you are looking down, you cannot see something that is above you." Pride separates you from the Lord and puts the focus on YOURSELF. If you want the fullest possible relationship with God, you must deal with the issue of pride in your life.

> **Though the LORD is exalted, He regards the lowly (and invites them into His fellowship); but the proud and haughty He knows at a distance.**
> *~Psalm 138:6* *(AMP)*

Pride is very sneaky. Pride doesn't want to be noticed. We often don't recognize when it's active in our minds. We justify what we're feeling and believing, so it doesn't *feel* like pride.

> **The heart is deceitful above all things and it is extremely sick; who can understand it fully and know its secret motives?**
> *~Jeremiah 17:9* *(AMP)*

Below is a list with examples of pride. As you read through them, ask yourself if you can relate to any of them. Be aware of your subconscious thoughts. Check the ones that are highlighted to you. Sit with the Lord, inviting Him to show you the areas within your own heart that need to be exposed and healed. Ask Him to show you where you have felt "superior" or "better than" other people. You will be given the opportunity to do a Value Exchange for them later in the chapter.

Examples of pride:

1. You put someone down in your mind (or with your mouth) because they insulted you and caused you to feel "put down."

2. You are not "teachable" because you already know everything. You might not pay attention because "it's a waste" of your time. You don't need advice; you already know that.

3. You don't want to do a task that's "below you." "It's not my job to clean toilets or pick up trash."

4. You dominate conversations by talking a lot and interrupting others.

5. You're overly attentive to your physical appearance and don't hesitate to spend lots of money to look attractive. You spend a lot of time getting ready.

6. You don't like to submit to authority or someone else's leadership. You like to be the boss. You don't like to be told what to do. "I make better decisions. I could do it better."

7. You don't respond to "just anybody's" texts, emails, or phone calls—just the ones you value or those you want something from (money, support, etc.).

8. You easily find fault with people around you and correct them.

9. You find it hard to admit when you're wrong. If forced to apologize, you say, "If I've hurt you, I'm sorry, BUT YOU ..." to defend yourself.

10. You're unable to see opposing viewpoints. You are right, they are wrong. End of discussion.

11. "Because I deserve to do it my way."

12. You talk about the important people you know. Doing this helps you feel important, too. "Name dropping."

13. You look down on someone who is less educated/successful or attractive, etc.

14. You're judgmental of people who don't believe or do things the way you do. You criticize and cut them down.

15. You're argumentative and like to have the last word, which helps you feel more powerful and in control, and makes you look good.

16. You're not genuinely thankful because you take the credit for everything you accomplish. You do not recognize God's hand in your life.

17. You find yourself complaining because "I deserve better; this shouldn't be happening to me."

18. You worry about your reputation. "What will people think?" Pride wants to protect you from the feeling of shame that comes from looking bad in other people's eyes.

19. You get hurt if people don't notice or reward you for the nice things you've done for them.

20. You don't enjoy being with people who aren't "impressed" with you.

21. You avoid being around people you think are inferior to you.

22. You don't read the Bible or pray because you "don't need to."

23. You're controlling. You want people to listen to you and obey. "It's my way or the highway."

24. You like to leave a better impression of yourself than is honestly true. You act differently in public than you do in private/at home.

25. You get defensive when corrected. You can't receive "constructive criticism."

26. You try to be "perfect" so you can look good (perfectionism).

27. You're proud of your accomplishments and like to talk about them (work, sports, etc.).

28. You compliment people to get something from them (attention, favor, status, etc.).

29. You believe your church is the best (religious pride). You believe whatever organization you're involved with is better than others. Everything else fails by comparison.

30. You're offended when other people get attention and compliments for what they do or say instead of you.

31. You disregard the advice of others.

32. You're the exception.

33. You justify your mistakes instead of admitting you were wrong. In this way, you find it hard to repent of anything. You come with excuses instead.

34. You feel offended and personally attacked if someone has an opposing viewpoint to yours.

35. You can't relate to the needs of others. You can't see how your words and actions might hurt them. You don't consider their feelings because you're more concerned about your own comfort and needs.

36. You behave in ways to draw attention to yourself. You may be excessively friendly or dramatic so people will notice you.

Pride wants to control, lead, be heard, influence, and be right.

LIST OF BENEFITS:

1. **Self-protection:** Keeps me from being "shamed" and from "looking bad" to other people. Protects my reputation.

2. **Self-motivation:** Pride puts pressure on me to work harder and perform better. Pride might also cause me to give up doing something that I might not do well enough.

3. **Self-elevation:** By looking down on someone who hurt my feelings, I can feel better about myself. Pride says, "I'm a better person than they are."

4. **Self-elevation:** By being dramatic, excessively friendly and over-complementing other people ("brown-nosing"), I can look better and get more favor.

5. **Self-justice:** By talking negatively about someone, I can make them look bad to other people and get the satisfaction of getting even.

6. **Self-justice/Self-elevation:** Rather than admit any fault of my own, I defend myself (in my own mind or openly with other people) with a list of reasons why I didn't do anything wrong (self-justify).

7. **Self-comfort:** Pride reassures me that I'm a good person. I'm wise, important and valued. Whatever I need reassurance about, pride is more than happy to help me!

Example 1: A friend of yours did something to hurt your feelings. It felt like they were being inconsiderate. As a response, you start believing, "They don't really care about me. I must not matter to them." You have now taken on the belief, "I don't matter." This is where pride starts to kick in. You start thinking, "I would NEVER have done that to them." You're more considerate and sensitive than they are. You may start attacking their integrity to protect your own. This can progress to a place where you become so critical that you're unable to see anything good in them. You want to honor the Lord and forgive those who hurt you, but you don't know how.

The first step is to identify the feeling or belief. In this case, the belief is, "I don't matter." Then identify the coping mechanisms you've attached to this belief. In this case, you felt "torn down." Pride is there to "build you up." Pride tries to make you feel better, providing comfort by saying, "I didn't deserve that. They had no right to treat me that way. I've been a good friend to them." Pride will also want you to hold onto unforgiveness so you can put up a wall and protect your heart from being hurt again. Pride is also self-elevating and takes justice, causing you to think, "I'm a better person than they are. I would be more considerate. I would never do that to them."

A Value Exchange would look like the following:

Lord Jesus, I recognize I'm holding pride and unforgiveness toward my friend because of the belief that I don't matter. I'm using these things for protection, comfort, elevation, and to take justice. I ask forgiveness for doing this. I choose to break agreement with unforgiveness and pride and all their ungodly benefits. I command all demonic assignments connected to these things to go now, in Jesus' name! Lord Jesus, I ask You to clean this out for me and give me what You value in exchange.

Be sure to take time to receive from the Lord.

Remember to go back to the memory where you felt these things. See if it still feels true that you "don't matter." If there is peace, then you have gotten a great exchange!

Example 2: You're a person who is highly accomplished in your chosen profession. You have lots of respect in the community and you know it. You have a lot of connections with high-ranking people. You have an expectation that people will treat you with favor. However, one day, someone very close to you was hurt by your attitude of superiority and they confronted you in love. You suddenly realized they were right, feeling the conviction of Holy Spirit and the need to repent.

A Value Exchange would look like the following:

Lord Jesus, I recognize that I've been walking in pride, believing I'm entitled to be treated with respect and honor because I'm superior to others. Thank You, Holy Spirit, for exposing this to me. I'm sorry for the ways I've used pride to self-elevate and control my environment to feel safe. I choose now to break agreement with pride and all its ungodly benefits. I command all demonic assignments connected to this to go now, in Jesus' name! Lord Jesus, please clean this out for me and give me what You have in exchange.

Be sure to take time to receive from the Lord.

Check a memory where you know you were operating in pride. Does it still feel true that you are superior? If not, you've gotten a good exchange.

FALSE HUMILITY

False humility is a twisted form of pride, motivated by wanting to avoid looking bad in other people's eyes. For instance, you may deflect compliments so you don't appear prideful. When you can't receive a compliment, you are belittling God's gift in you. You may also talk about your deficiencies, even jokingly, so other people will tell you how good you are. Or you may repent again and again hoping to look holy, taking great pride in being "a sinner saved by grace. It's good to be a good sinner (in a religious sense)!" You may see yourself as humble because you're living out the "ideal and perfect" righteous life. You live below your means, proving how humble you are by having the perfect, "righteous" home, car, and clothing. In this way, you're keeping up the appearance of what you're convinced humility looks like.

Example 1: To avoid looking prideful, you have problems accepting compliments. Yet, when you avoid receiving a compliment, you find people become more assertive, trying to convince you that you deserve the accolade. This feels good, but you would never admit it because this would look prideful! Suddenly, you catch yourself doing this and realize you're using false humility to protect yourself from appearing prideful! Time for a Value Exchange!

Lord Jesus, I recognize I'm using false humility to protect myself from appearing prideful. I'm sorry and ask Your forgiveness for doing this. I now choose to break agreement with false humility and give up its ungodly protection. I command all demonic assignments connected to this to go now, in Jesus' name! Lord Jesus, I ask You to clean this out for me and give me what You have in exchange.

Be sure to take time to receive from the Lord.

Be sure to check a memory where you know you've used false humility. How does it feel to accept a compliment now? If it feels good, you've just gotten a Kingdom perspective!

True humility is the exact opposite of humanism. Rather than ignoring the existence of God, humility recognizes that every good thing about you and everything you have to give originates with God. True humility will give God the glory, and you will have the joy of partnering with Him!

So, as God's own chosen people, who are holy (set apart, sanctified for His purpose) and well-beloved (by God Himself), put on a heart of compassion, kindness, humility, gentleness, and patience (which has the power to endure whatever injustice or unpleasantness comes, with good temper); bearing graciously with one another, and willingly forgiving each other if one has a cause for complaint against another; just as the Lord has forgiven you, so should you forgive.
~Colossians 3:12 *(AMP)*

Prayer:

I come before You, Jesus, as a willing and humble servant. I ask for Your strength, encouragement, and wisdom to carry out the destiny that You have called me to. I desire with all my heart to honor You and may all the works that I do in Your name bring You glory. For I'm aware that without Your help, I'm destined to fail. But I choose to embrace the truth of Your Word that says, "I can do all things through Christ who strengthens me!" Oh, Lord, thank You for Your provision that will provide all I need to honor You in all my ways. I love You, Jesus! In Your holy name I pray, Amen.

CHAPTER 11

THE INJUSTICES OF LIFE

Injustice is a part of life. At some point, either socially or personally, we have all felt the pain of injustice coming from life experiences being unfair and wrong. In contrast, fairness makes us happy and satisfied, even when it's for someone else. Injustice is either a violation of what is perceived as morally right or a violation of the rights of another. This often causes feelings of being slighted or cheated, which can progress into grumbling, resentment, bitterness, anger, frustration, helplessness, sadness, and even vengeance! It is the "mad-sad" cycle!

Ongoing injustice where "nothing ever changes" often results in feeling "like a victim." In these circumstances, you may take on a "me against them" attitude. Unfortunately, if you have this attitude, your sensitivity to injustice will cause you to search for every little thing you perceive is unjust. In this way, you're amplifying every injustice, which makes it feel even worse. Your only escape may be to fantasize about finding a way out of the situation.

Injustice may trigger anger ("fight") and/or fear ("flight") responses. Anger will cause you to obsess over offenses, putting blame on people who hurt you. Anger will demand justice, wanting revenge with a goal of causing the other person(s) to feel the repercussion for their actions. You may fantasize about taking revenge, finding creative ways to make the other person(s) *pay* or bring justice to whatever you feel is wrong. Anger may cause you to overreact, disrupt, or end relationships. You may realize you're sabotaging important relationships by your behaviors, which might cause shame and guilt about what you've done. Anger can feel like it gives you power to assert your voice, demanding justice.

Fear of injustice might cause you to avoid situations and conflict, keeping you "on your guard." Or you may become a "good prisoner." This will cause you to "suck it up," holding your tongue (giving up your voice), submit (be quiet, holding it in), and obey to avoid "making waves." In this way, you "give up, give in and give out" with the hope of earning approval.

True freedom is being able to think, act, and react from a place of wisdom and peace that is determined by understanding and aligning oneself with the perspective of Jesus. Instead, we have a compulsion to act out of the perspective of our emotions, allowing them to determine our truth. This influences our perspective and motivates us to seek self-preservation. The truth that sets you free is the PERSPECTIVE OF GOD!

If this victim mentality persists long enough, it may become attached to your identity. Without realizing it, you try to get some benefit out of negative situation(s). You're a victim of an unjust "system"—a place of negativity where "I just exist." When this happens, you'll view life with an expectation of injustices happening to you. At this point, you feel powerless and helpless, believing things will never change, and you might as well accept that fact. With the victim mentality, you'll feel "owned and controlled" by family, friends, institutions, etc.

Finding freedom feels like it is dependent on circumstances changing to your liking and expectations. Corrie ten Boom was a Holocaust death-camp victim who *lived free*, despite the profound injustice of her circumstances. She did this by keeping her eyes on Jesus, trusting Him for strength, well-being, and peace. In Him, she was able to stand in a horrific trial, never blaming God, but trusting in Him. She stated, "Never be afraid to trust an unknown future to a known God."

True freedom is being able to think, act, and react from a place of wisdom and peace that is determined by understanding and aligning oneself with the perspective of Jesus. Instead, we have a compulsion to act out of the perspective of our emotions, allowing them to determine our truth. This influences our perspective and motivates us to seek self-preservation. The truth that sets you free is the PERSPECTIVE OF GOD!

What's your definition of justice? We tend to have an idea of what justice should look like—to satisfy our need for justice and "to make them pay." Anything less than that perspective doesn't *feel* like true justice. You may think you'll be free of injustice when the other person sincerely apologizes, trying to make amends. You may think justice is served when they get in trouble for how they treated you. You may think justice is served when your friends support you and turn against the person(s) involved. And the list goes on and on.

This is a good place to ask the Lord what justice looks like from His perspective.

> **He has told you, O man, what is good; and what does the LORD require of you Except to be just, and to love (and diligently practice) kindness (compassion), And to walk humbly with your God (setting aside any overblown sense of importance or self-righteousness)?**
> ~*Micah 6:8* (AMP)

Regardless of what anybody else is doing, we're supposed to act justly. That will cost you all the benefits and coping mechanisms listed below. You need to get the Value Exchanges necessary to be able to love from a place of grace and mercy. In this way, we look like Jesus and have taken on the identity of Christ. We trust Holy Spirit to guard our hearts and minds, regardless of our circumstances and what other people think of us. Nobody can put you into bondage unless you give them power to do so.

When you carry injustice, you become "yoked" to the offense and the person who offended you. This connection is negative and will negatively influence how you think and act. This negative has become your truth. You could be yoked to Jesus instead! You need to let go of the injustice and choose to be yoked to Him!

> **For the LORD is (absolutely) righteous, He loves righteousness (virtue, morality, justice); The upright shall see His face.**
> *~Psalm 11:7* (AMP)

The possible values of injustice include the following:

All these self-motivated benefits involve the desire to bring justice or justify your reactions to the situation.

1. **Self-justice/self-elevation/control:** I use anger to try to bring justice and make my voice heard.

2. **Self-protection:** I put up a wall against the people responsible for the injustice.

3. **Self-protection:** I withdraw and give up trying. "It's not worth fighting because there's no way to win."

4. **Self-motivation/self-elevation:** I feel the need to always defend myself (self-justifying) to other people by stating my case, which makes me look better in their eyes.

5. **Self-motivation:** I feel the urge to find ways to make things just. I find that I can't let the injustice go until things are made right. Letting the injustice go would feel unjust, and justice would not be served.

6. **Self-comfort:** Feeling like a "victim" because of the injustice causes me to say or do things (like emotionally acting out) to get sympathy and affirmation from others with the goal of feeling better about myself.

7. **Self-elevation/self-justice:** Rather than forgiving, I hold an unrighteous judgement against the people involved by looking down on them for what they did. I feel better by judging their character.

8. **Self-justice:** I feel good when I can manipulate circumstances to "make them pay for what they did." I may make them feel guilty or publicly shame them "because that's what they deserve." Or I may keep them punished in my mind.

9. **Self-comfort:** By giving up, I can "lick my wounds" in peace, feeling sorry for myself.

10. **Self-comfort:** I can fantasize about what it would look like for justice to be served.

11. **Self-comfort/self-justice:** It feels good (comforting) to be angry about the injustice.

12. **Self-elevation:** Anger validates my feelings (telling me that I'm right). I give myself a "stamp of approval."

13. **Self-elevation/self-justice/self-comfort/control:** I may rebel (an act of violent or open resistance to authority or control) to *feel* like I'm doing something about the injustice. In this way, I'm trying to "force a change" and may even get a type of high from the act itself. This helps me feel in control. Being in control and knowing I'm doing something about a perceived wrong is comforting.

Example 1: Injustice often starts in childhood. For example, you may have felt like a sibling got more attention than you. You may also have noticed you had to work hard for privileges whereas your sibling got them handed over, sending a message that you're "less than" them. The injustice of this caused you to be resentful and angry. Eventually you gave up trying to bring justice. You become a victim to this situation that you can't change. In this way, you know how to "be" or exist, using the least amount of effort on your part with less pushback from your parents. This feeling of being a victim has followed you into your adult life. Nothing ever appears to go your way. Everyone else always gets the favor. Despite your best efforts, the injustice continues. You realize you're stuck in a cycle of victim mentality and in need of healing.

A Value Exchange would look something like this:

> *Lord Jesus, I recognize I've been holding onto injustice and have walked in a victim mentality because of it. I also have taken on the belief that I'm "less than" others. I have used these beliefs to self-comfort and protect myself because I "know how to be." I confess I've used anger and resentment to gain control, self-elevate, and feel vindicated. I'm sorry and ask your forgiveness for doing this. I now choose to break agreement with injustice, victim mentality, and everything attached to it. I choose to give up all their ungodly benefits. I command all demonic assignments connected to these things to go now, in Jesus' name! Lord Jesus, I ask you to please clean this out for me and give me what You value in exchange.*

Be sure to take time to receive from the Lord.

Now check a memory where you felt injustice. Does it still feel true that you need to be angry or resentful? Do you still feel like a victim? If not, then you have gotten an amazing Value Exchange resulting in a Kingdom perspective! If you still feel the sting of injustice, then address other possible attached benefits or beliefs.

Example 2: You got hired into an office for the current rate of pay for that time period. After several years, you realize new people coming into your same position are making more than you because there has been a shortage of people to fill your position. You bring this to your supervisor's attention, but they tell you your pay can't be changed. Quitting isn't an option because of financial needs. You find yourself angry, complaining to friends, and putting the company down. You're sad and frustrated from feeling not valued. You find yourself daydreaming a lot about your boss recognizing your value and giving you a raise or getting revenge by suing them. You realize the only way to happiness and freedom is to let go of the injustice.

Your Value Exchange would look something like this:

Lord Jesus, I recognize I've been holding onto injustice, sadness, and not feeling valued. I've used these things to justify my anger as a way to self-elevate by complaining and putting down the company. I've also used daydreaming/fantasy to comfort myself and bring a sense of justice. Please forgive me. I now choose to break agreement with injustice and not feeling valued and give up the benefits connected to them. I break off all demonic assignments connected to these things and command them to go now, in Jesus' name! Lord Jesus, I ask You to clean this out for me and please give me what You value in exchange.

Be sure to take time to receive from the Lord.

Check a memory where you know you felt injustice. Do you still feel the pain of not being valued? Do you still feel angry, frustrated, and sad? If you're feeling peace and forgiveness, then you are set free!

Prayer:

Papa, excite my ears! I choose to be purposeful in my pursuit of listening to Your amazing voice of love. Your voice is so kind and gentle. Never condemning, always guiding, and encouraging me to come up higher. Thank You, Jesus, for I know You are always pursuing me and You never give up!

CHAPTER 12

JEALOUSY AND ENVY

JEALOUSY

Jealousy between people is a complex emotion that is aroused when you perceive a fear or threat of losing something or someone. It can be found in boyfriend/girlfriend or parent/child relationships, marriage, friendships, between co-workers, etc. This emotion is fear-based, arising from feeling insecure, and can range from mental uneasiness and suspicion to bitterness, resentment, and anger against the person whom you feel is trying to take something or someone away from you.

> **You are still worldly (controlled by ordinary impulses, the sinful capacity). For as long as there is jealously and strife and discord among you, are you not unspiritual, and are you not walking like ordinary men (unchanged by faith)?**
> *~1 Corinthians 3:3* *(AMP)*

The possible values of jealousy include the following:

1. **Self-protection:** Alerts me to the danger of losing something valuable—a relationship, position, etc. This gets me ready for the "blow" of loss.

2. **Self-protection:** Causes me to "put a guard up" with the people involved.

3. **Self-motivation:** Compels me to take steps to protect my relationship or possession(s).

4. **Self-motivation:** Arouses suspicion, causing me to monitor another person's actions and whereabouts.

5. **Self-motivation/self-elevation:** Causes me to take actions to perform better, earning my place or position, hoping to feel more secure.

6. **Self-elevation:** I can judge, look down on, and/or gossip about the person who poses the threat to feel better about myself.

7. **Self-justice:** I confront the person causing me to feel threatened. I may also threaten the person I'm afraid of losing, giving an ultimatum ("You will do this, or else!") to correct and control their actions.

8. **Self-comfort:** Knowing I'm "on top of the situation" is very satisfying.

Example 1: You're a supervisor in a company. You hire someone, only to find out later they excel beyond your own skills. You begin to feel threatened because the boss has taken notice of them and is really impressed. You become suspicious and fearful you're losing your favor and are now in danger of losing your position. The "red flag" of jealously rises up and now you're angry. You worked hard for this position and are NOT going to lose it to some brown-noser! This threat is always on your mind. You're motivated to find ways to look better and make them look worse. Eventually you take steps to confront your rival, letting them know who's boss. You begin to recognize you're miserable and you're negatively affecting your work environment. Now you're ready to take steps to receive the healing you need to move forward in a positive direction.

A Value Exchange might look like this:

> *Lord Jesus, I recognize I've been feeling jealous. I've used it to motivate myself to work harder to be better than my rival. I've used it to self-protect by raising my guard and being diligent to watch their every move. I've used self-elevation by putting them down. I've taken justice by making sure they know their place. I ask forgiveness for doing this. I now choose to break agreement with jealousy and give up all the value I have place on it. I command all demonic assignments connected to this to go, in Jesus' name! Lord Jesus, I ask that You clean this out for me and give me what You have in exchange.*

Be sure to take time to receive from the Lord.

Remember to go back into a memory where you had been feeling jealous. Do you still feel uneasy or threatened with jealousy? If it feels peaceful, then you have success!

Example 2: You've been in a long-time relationship with your significant other. You know they've been intimate with another person in the past. As you are browsing Facebook, you see they've friended that other person and are now "liking" some of their posts. Now the "red flag" of jealousy's warning comes up. You become fearful and start to wonder if something is going on between them. You start monitoring their phone, looking for any suspicious activity. Your mind starts creating possible scenarios of what you think is happening. You're motivated to try harder to please your mate, making sure they're happy with you. You cater to their every anticipated need. Eventually you confront them. They reassure you of their love and dedication to you. But you have a hard time believing them. You demand they "unfriend" the person. But even once they've done that, you don't feel any better. Nothing they do seems to have the power to convince you. When you're fearful like this, you are unable to trust. At some point, you realize how irrational you're being. You see the strain your actions are causing in your relationship and are motivated to make a change.

A Value Exchange may look like this:

Lord Jesus, I recognize that I've taken on jealousy. I've used it to protect myself by putting up my guard, being hypervigilant in monitoring the actions of my mate. I've used it to motivate myself by finding ways to please them, so they'll be happy with me. I've used it to bring justice by confronting them. I've tried to control them by demanding they unfriend the person so I can feel secure. I ask forgiveness for doing this. I choose to break agreement with jealousy and all its benefits. I command all demonic assignments connected to this to go, in Jesus' name! Lord Jesus, I ask that You clean this out for me and give me what You have in exchange.

Be sure to take time to receive from the Lord.

Remember to go back into a memory where you had felt jealous. Do you still feel consumed with jealousy? Do you feel you need to suspiciously monitor your mate? If you think about the other person, do you have any fear or uneasiness? If it feels peaceful, then you have success!

ENVY

Envy involves being painfully aware of another's advantage over you, causing you to look at them with "ill will" and "eye them maliciously." It's a resentful, dissatisfied longing for what other people possess or have achieved, that you don't have. This can include physical appearance, finances, possessions, attributes, status, intelligence, etc. You've compared yourself to someone else and found yourself lacking. You "want what they have," and having it would give you greater happiness or value. Not having it would cause you to feel "less than" and lacking. In doing this, you've "idolized" a certain attribute you feel you lack, and you won't be satisfied until you attain it.

This is a never-ending quest because no matter how much you achieve, you're always on the lookout for someone who has "more." There is always someone with more popularity or a higher position or better than you. You continue to aim higher and higher, always changing the "target" that would make you feel successful or satisfied. But attaining the reward doesn't always have the pay-off you thought it would. You are not satisfied.

Love endures with patience and serenity, love is kind and thoughtful, and is not jealous or envious; love does not brag and is not proud or arrogant.
~1 Corinthians 13:4 *(AMP)*

The possible values of envy include the following:

1. **Self-protection:** My painful awareness of not being able to attain what someone else has causes me to push them away, protecting myself from feeling lack and/or having less worth.

2. **Self-motivation:** I try to find a way to match or excel so I have what they have.

3. **Self-elevation:** I fantasize about how it would look and feel if I possessed what I desire.

4. **Self-elevation/self-justice:** By thinking or talking badly about the person I envy, I'm "lowering" them to feel better about myself and taking justice because they deserve it.

5. **Self-justice:** I fantasize about the many ways they could lose what they have because, "It's not fair and they don't deserve it." This could lead to violent thoughts, which may in extreme cases, progress to violent acts.

6. **Self-comfort:** By using all the above, I'm comforted, knowing I'm doing something about the situation and my feelings of lack.

Example 1: You love Christmas! You spent a lot of money decorating with lights and Christmas decorations. You got lots of attention and felt you were bringing enjoyment to people. Other people started decorating for Christmas also. The next Christmas, your neighbors put up a bigger display with more creative decorations than you, directing the attention away from you. Everyone in the community is driving by their house to look at their amazing light show. Your decorations pale in comparison. You become green with envy but realize you can't compete financially to buy more decorations. Envy would say, "This was MY idea. What gives them the right to copy me?" You start to feel bitter, resentful, and start avoiding them. You HATE it when people compliment them! You start to fantasize about ways you could sabotage their display. You point out the flaws in their display and character to put them down. Your spouse tells you to "get over it already" because you're getting harder to live with and it's all you talk about. You suddenly come to your senses and realize you have gone too far.

A Value Exchange may look like this:

> *Lord Jesus, I recognize I've become envious of my neighbor. I've used envy, bitterness, and resentment to help me avoid them and to protect myself. I've used fantasy to take justice and motivate me to think of ways to "even the score." I put them down to self-elevate and help me feel better about myself. I ask forgiveness for doing this. I now choose to break agreement with envy, bitterness, and resentment and all the ungodly values I've placed on them. I command all demonic assignments connected to this to go, in Jesus' name! Lord Jesus, I ask You to clean this place out for me and give me what You have in exchange.*

Be sure to take time to receive from the Lord.

Remember to test your healing by putting yourself into a memory where you felt envy, bitterness, and resentment. How does it feel now? If you're not feeling peace, then identify the emotion/belief you're feeling and then address it with another Value Exchange.

Example 2: You have a best friend who seems to have good fortune follow them in whatever endeavor they engage in. They excelled in sports, school, and business. On top of that, they have the audacity to be very good looking! On the other hand, you hit several walls and challenges involving finances; a business deal falls through and you lose your job. During this series of unfortunate events, your friend keeps excelling! Envy begins to rear its ugly head. This is unfair! What did you do to deserve this? What did they do to deserve the good fortune?! Now you're getting angry. In your envy, you start to avoid them because they remind you of everything wrong in your life and the injustice of it all. You get snippy with your friend when they tell you about their latest accomplishment. Envy says, "They think they're so perfect" and so you start finding things about them that are "flawed" to help you feel better about yourself. Your friend begins to question you because they sense your negativity and can feel you pulling away from them. They help you realize they've done nothing wrong and that your misfortune is not their fault.

A Value Exchange may look like this:

> Lord Jesus, I recognize I've become envious of my best friend. I avoid them to protect me from feeling bad about myself. I criticize them, looking for "flaws" to help me feel better about myself. I'm using anger to help me avoid them. Envy tells me they're prideful, and so I respond by using "snippiness" as a countermeasure to bring justice. This is comforting because I've done something about the injustice. I ask forgiveness for doing these things. I choose to break agreement with envy and all its attached benefits. I command all demonic assignments connected to these things to go now, in Jesus' name. Lord Jesus, I ask You to clean this out for me and give me what You have in exchange.

Be sure to take time to receive from the Lord.

Remember to put yourself in a memory involving your friend to see if you still feel envious. Does it still feel true that "they think they're so perfect?" Does this still feel unfair? Do you still see all their "flaws"? If you don't feel peace, then identify the emotion and belief and do another Value Exchange.

But if you have bitter jealousy and selfish ambition in your hearts, do not be arrogant, and (as a result) be in defiance of the truth. This (superficial) wisdom is not that which comes down from above, but is earthly (secular), natural (unspiritual), even demonic. For where jealousy and selfish ambition exist, there is disorder (unrest, rebellion) and every evil thing and morally degrading practice.
~James 3:14-16 (AMP)

Prayer:

Father, I love You so very much! My eyes flood with tears when I sit in Your presence. I love beholding You and the wonders that are expressed through Your Son, Jesus. How I long for more of You! Jesus, cause me to keep my eyes fixed on You. Help me in my busyness to remember to connect with Your love and allow You to strengthen me. Holy Spirit, help me. Draw me to Truth! Expose my weaknesses and grow them into Kingdom truths! Help me to be a fisher of men. Help me to cast my net, believing for a catch. Help me to trust You and give me confidence to step out in boldness, not worrying about my own reputation. Fill me with radical love for You, God, and for Your people—putting others first and being Jesus in all situations. I love You, God. Help me to be a better lover.

CHAPTER 13

SADNESS

Sadness can be described as a feeling of being downcast, unhappy, or grieved. It's a deep, inner feeling of emotional pain which might feel heavy, crushing, or even disabling. Unfortunately, there are many things in life that can cause feelings of sadness, including a harsh word from a friend, the death of a loved one, the loss of a job, chronic disease, or pain in the body, and so forth. There is sadness when we feel forgotten, left out, rejected, betrayed, lonely, or disappointed. We experience sadness and weariness when we're in circumstances that never seem to get better despite believing and praying for breakthrough. It is incredibly sad when our children or spouses wander away from the Lord. We want to feel loved, cherished, and valued. So, we struggle with sadness when those desires are not met. Even David struggled with sadness as below:

> **Why are you in despair, O my soul? And why are you restless and disturbed within me? Hope in God and wait expectantly for Him, for I shall again praise Him, the help of my (sad) countenance and my God.**
> ~Psalm 43:5 *(AMP)*

We live in a world with wounded people who, in turn, wound other people. We have all been insensitive and hurt others as well. The more intimate we are with someone, the more risk there is of being hurt when something goes wrong. In the moment of being hurt, there is a *true* sadness that needs to be addressed. However, if we hold the pain in our heart, the wound will grow and become even more painful. It is important to learn how to release the sadness right away. When pain is not released, it gets heavy and progresses into other emotional issues like depression, hopelessness, despair, etc.

A healthy way to deal with sadness is to acknowledge that what happened is *truly sad*. Whatever happened to hurt you is "not okay," whether it was intentional, unintentional, or a physical illness. God is not okay with the fact you're suffering, either emotionally or physically. You don't have to brush it off and say, "It's okay" when it's not. Praise God, there is a way to release sadness!!

Initially, all sadness starts as *truth based*, because whatever happened was sad. When this sadness is not released, then you'll start taking on coping mechanisms to help deal with it.

TRUTH-BASED SADNESS

Example 1: Let's say you lost your spouse, child, parent, or best friend recently through death. This loss is devastating, and sadness hits you to the core, carrying with it a deep pain and sense of loss that feels as though it cannot be filled. It is important for us to understand that Jesus came to carry our pain and sorrow, so we CAN lay our burden of sadness in His hands and release it. Do this daily as you walk through the grieving process. This takes time, but have patience for yourself in this journey. In doing this, it will keep the pain of loss and sadness from becoming a heavy burden, allowing you to grieve in a healthy way.

When giving truth-based sadness to Jesus, picture yourself holding out your arms toward Him, palms up, and *intentionally* releasing the pain. Or you could picture yourself handing Jesus your sad heart. In either case, allow yourself to FEEL the pain and sadness lift off you.

A Value Exchange prayer might go something like this:

Jesus, I choose to give You permission to take this pain and sadness away. I acknowledge the sadness I'm feeling is true. I don't want to hold onto it and carry its burden. I ask You to take it and give me what You have for me in exchange.

Be sure to take time to receive from the Lord.

Remember to check yourself afterwards to see if the intensity of sadness feels better.

Example 2: Occasionally, after receiving a Value Exchange for a negative emotion/belief, you go back into the memory to check and see if it is still present and feels true. You find it no longer feels true, but you still feel intense sadness. The sadness is no longer attached to any belief other than the fact that what happened was sad. While it will always be true that what happened is sad, you don't have to carry the pain of sadness. The prayer will be the same as above.

Keep your heart in a place of *receiving*. Let Him do that exchange for you. He loves you and joyfully restores your heart.

> **As for those who grieve over Zion, God has sent Me to give them a beautiful crown in exchange for ashes, to anoint them with gladness instead of sorrow; to wrap them in victory, joy, and praise instead of depression and sadness.**
> *~Isaiah 61:3* (VOICE)

LIE-BASED SADNESS

When there is repeated wounding of your heart, you may start believing lies about yourself or God. For instance, if you're constantly left out and put down by others, you may start believing you are worthless, rejected, and alone. Sadness is attached to all these beliefs. *You will act out what you believe about yourself and sadness will be your constant companion.*

For example, if during kindergarten you didn't feel like you fit in with other kids in your class, you would be sad about that. As you try to figure out why, you could take on the belief, "I'm not good enough" and feel rejected. You could further decide there's something intrinsically wrong or bad about you compared to other people. At this point, you may feel ashamed of yourself. This can all lead to God-based beliefs in which you now conclude, "God must not love me since He made me this wrong and bad way."

The longer you hold onto these lie-based beliefs about yourself or God, the more likely you'll be to attach other negative emotions to the original sadness. The same applies to the emotions connected to ongoing chronic illness and diseases. There is sadness in all types of suffering. The progression of sadness and grief can lead to feelings of discouragement, emptiness, depression, hopelessness, feeling defeated, despair, and the like. Without healing, these emotions can develop into self-condemnation and/or self-hatred, which can lead to self-harm and thoughts of suicide. As you see, you can start with sadness and end up with suicide. This is like an infection that's not responding to your coping skills.

All these thoughts are negative and cause your mind to get wired in a negative default. The brain will automatically think negatively, and you'll live out of that mindset. Just like other negative emotions, your subconscious mind will develop coping and defense mechanisms to deal with them. The Value Exchange can change the negative default and put in place a Truth-based pathway. Jesus has a legal right to do this because of the sacrifice He made on the Cross for you.

Let the peace of Christ (the inner calm of one who walks daily with Him) be the controlling factor in your hearts (deciding and settling questions that arise). To this peace indeed you were called as members in one body (of believers). And be thankful (to God always).
~Colossians 3:15 (AMP)

> The Value Exchange can change the negative default and put in place a Truth-based pathway. Jesus has a legal right to do this because of the sacrifice He made on the Cross for you.

The first step would be to identify what is making you sad.

Do this by asking yourself the following questions:

1. When did I first notice I was feeling sad?
2. What happened that would have caused me to feel sad?
3. What message did that moment "send" to me about myself?
4. Was it the belief that made me sad?
5. Does that belief still feel true to me?

For example, you might remember walking into church one Sunday and perceive a group of friends ignoring you, which made you sad. This sent a message to you that you were "dissed" and not important to them. This belief, "I'm not important," feels true. By asking the above questions, you now have identified the belief behind the emotion.

The next step would be to identify the coping mechanisms you've attached to sadness.

Possible coping mechanisms would be the following:

1. **Self-protection:** If I stay sad, I'll cushion the blow of the next sad thing.

2. **Self-protection:** I can put on an act and be cheerful around the people who hurt me, keeping them from knowing they hurt me. This avoids confrontation and protects me from appearing weak.

3. **Self-protection:** Putting up a wall of protection keeps people "at a distance" so they can't hurt me.

4. **Self-protection:** I avoid doing activities that might be "risky," but it also gets me out of doing things I don't feel like doing.

5. **Self-motivation/self-protection:** Sadness helps me know how to think, adjust to, and accept a sad situation I can't change. It's easier to just *stay sad* than to try to feel better.

6. **Self-motivation:** Motivates me to find the strength within *myself* to help make it through (existing, but not thriving) a sad circumstance that doesn't change. In doing this, I'm relying solely on myself instead of God's strength.

7. **Self-motivation:** I can use sadness as fuel, causing me to work harder to help find ways to change the circumstances that caused the sadness.

8. **Self-motivation/self-elevation/self-comfort:** I tell everyone how horribly I was treated to get attention and pity.

9. **Self-justice:** I outwardly express my sadness around the person who hurt me to cause them to feel guilty and punish them for what they did. I refuse to accept any apologies, with the intent of making them feel more guilty.

10. **Self-comfort:** I use self-pity to be comforted because nobody else is comforting me.

11. **Self-comfort:** I hold onto the sadness caused by the death of a loved one to help me feel connected to them, which feels comforting to me. Letting go of this would feel like I'm betraying their memory or that I might forget them. (See the chapter on Soul Ties.)

12. **Self-comfort:** I may turn to sugar, food, alcohol, or other substances to help me feel better. I also might go on shopping sprees to feel better. These coping mechanisms may become an addiction. If so, see the Addictions chapter.

13. **Self-comfort:** Taking on thoughts of suicide gives me a way out of the sadness and may give some form of comfort and hope. Not having a way out feels out of control and hopeless. It's comforting to know I have the option of suicide.

As you read the examples, try to identify the coping mechanisms used and what a Value Exchange might look like.

Example 1: As a married adult, you've experienced much *disappointment*. Your hopes and dreams of raising a family turned out different than what actually happened. One child was born with disabilities. There were communication difficulties between you and your spouse. Your children were strong willed and made wrong choices. There was frequent conflict in the home. Initially, you tried really hard to make things better, pushing yourself to find solutions. But it didn't work and you feel out of control. This is not the "ideal" family life you thought it would be. Your mind struggles with how to think and not be overcome by sadness. It becomes hard to see the positive about anything anymore. You find yourself focusing on the negative, which is just plain sad. Eventually, there isn't a lot you find enjoyment in, and you gradually slip into depression. In this depression, you find comfort in food or alcohol, which helps numb the pain. You withdraw emotionally by putting up "walls" around your family to avoid being hurt as badly.

What is it you're feeling that's making you sad?

In this case, you're feeling intense disappointment.

What coping mechanisms have you attached to the sadness and disappointment?

1. They can motivate you to be proactive in finding solutions that would bring a change.

2. When nothing changes after trying harder to improve family dynamics, eventually you give up. It feels easier to just stay in that "sad place" than try to get out of it. This keeps you from feeling as disappointed because you know what to expect.

3. Sinking into depression causes you to feel sorry for yourself (self-pity).

4. Now you stuff yourself full of chocolate and donuts and wine for comfort and to feel in control of *something* (refer to the Addictions chapter).

5. You emotionally withdraw, putting up walls to protect your heart.

A Value Exchange might look like this:

> *Lord Jesus, I recognize I've been holding onto sadness and disappointment and have used them to motivate myself and help me know how to think and what to expect in this sad situation. I've used the depression connected to it for comfort and to feel more in control. I've put up walls to protect my heart from being hurt. I ask Your forgiveness for doing these things. I choose to break agreement with sadness, disappointment, and depression and all their ungodly benefits. I command all demonic assignments connected to these things to go now, in Jesus' name! Lord Jesus, I ask You to please clean these things out for me and give me what You value in exchange.*

Be sure to take time to receive from the Lord.

Remember to check a memory and see if the sadness and disappointment are still present. If there is a feeling of peace, then you have gotten a good exchange!

Example 2: As a child, you found yourself never able to please the adults in your life no matter how hard you tried. Initially, you tried to work harder to prove yourself, but you eventually gave up. You were *never* "good enough" and *never* "measured up" to their standards. As you grew up, you became hyperaware of criticism. This kept you "on the alert," noticing every raised eyebrow and "hint" of negativity toward you, always expecting to be criticized and judged as "not good enough." Every time this happens, it feels like *evidence*, convincing you it's true.

Now you start taking on the belief that something is *definitely wrong* with you. This *evidence* not only proves you're "not good enough" and will never "measure up," but now you also believe "something is wrong with me" and "I don't belong." This adds to the pain. This becomes overwhelmingly hopeless, and you see no way out. You start to look for a way out and suicide becomes tempting. You already tried everything else. You can't change other people and there doesn't appear to be any other answer. Suicide would be the *easiest* way to escape the pain.

By this time, you've also put up "walls" of protection around your heart to avoid being hurt by other people. You've become fearful of doing things that would put you at risk for being shamed and humiliated, and you avoid putting yourself "out there" in situations where you would feel vulnerable. You finally decide to get help for this overwhelming sadness.

The first question to ask yourself would be, "What am I feeling that's making me sad?"

You're feeling sad because of the beliefs that you are "not good enough," you'll never measure up, something is hopelessly wrong with you, and you don't belong.

What coping mechanisms have you attached to the sadness and the beliefs?

1. The sadness was initially a motivator to try to prove yourself.

2. The sadness motivated you to be "hyperaware" of criticism and "on the alert," to be protected from being not good enough and not measuring up. In this situation, you're proactively "looking for" perceived signs from others that you're not good enough so that you can avoid them.

3. The sadness has now moved into a state of hopelessness, and you have entertained thoughts of suicide as a way out. This gives you hope that there is a way to find peace.

4. The sadness has caused you to put up a wall of protection around your heart to avoid getting hurt. You don't let people get too close to you.

5. The sadness has caused you to avoid participating in activities that seem too risky.

A Value Exchange might look like this:

Lord Jesus, I recognize I've been holding onto sadness and the beliefs that I'm not good enough, I will never measure up, something is hopelessly wrong with me, and I don't belong. I realize I've used these things for self-protection and to motivate me to try harder to earn acceptance. I also have entertained thoughts of suicide as a way out of my pain. I ask forgiveness for doing this. I choose now to break agreement with sadness and everything I have attached to it. I command all demonic assignments connected to these things to go now, in Jesus' name! Lord Jesus, I ask that You please clean this out for me and give me what You have in exchange.

Be careful to take time to receive from the Lord.

Remember to check a memory to see if those beliefs and their sadness are gone. What do you feel and believe now in those places?

**Come to Me, all who are weary and burdened,
and I will give you rest.**
~Matthew 11:28 (VOICE)

Prayer:

Papa, I love You so much! My heart yearns to draw closer to You. Peace is found only under the shadow of Your wings. You are my conqueror and my confidence! Reclaim Your created purpose for my life! Work Your fullness in me so that I radiate with Your light of glory in me! Cause me to walk in the pleasures of Your good and perfect will!

CHAPTER 14

ADDICTIONS

An addiction is a condition in which you have become *physically and emotionally dependent* on a particular substance or doing a particular thing or activity. To stop taking the substance or doing that particular activity would cause adverse effects. Addictions are chronic and persistent behaviors people continue to do despite negative consequences. These behaviors are an effort to control or avoid discomfort at some level. Certain pleasurable behaviors affect the same reward centers of the brain as drugs that are abused, becoming an acceptable way of dealing with life. Lasting changes will only happen when you find out what's driving you to seek comfort or pleasure through addicted behavior. You do this by figuring out the emotions and beliefs connected to it.

Synonyms for addiction include: dependency, fixation, weakness, compulsion, and enslavement. By asking yourself these questions, you can identify what you could possibly be addicted to:

1. What am I dependent on for my well-being or to help me cope?

2. What am I fixated on? What grabs my attention and helps me escape?

3. Where do I feel helpless, weak, or unable to control an area of my life?

4. Am I feeling compelled (forced) to do something?

5. Is there anything in my life where I feel enslaved?

Examples of addictions include: sugar, caffeine, alcohol, tobacco, vaping, marijuana, cocaine, heroin, pain medications (Norco, Morphine), benzodiazepines (like Xanax), stimulants (Ritalin, Adderall, meth), sedatives (barbiturates like Fiornal), inhalants (glue, gasoline, household cleaning products/aerosols), food, pornography, fantasy, sex, exercise, body building, tanning, cosmetic surgery, tattooing, piercings, shopping, playing video games ("gaming"), thumb sucking, work ("workaholism"), being on social media/phones, gambling.

The brain is very imaginative, and so the possibilities for addictions are endless and unique to each person.

Signs of addiction:

1. Feeling a deep need to do the behavior.

2. Not feeling like yourself unless you're doing the behavior.

3. Having a panic/anxiety reaction if unable to do the behavior.

4. Finding yourself thinking about the behavior most of the time.

5. Arranging your life around the behavior.

All types of addictions have the possibility of progressing. For example, marijuana is considered a gateway drug that leads to using other drugs to get a better high. Narcotics are a gateway drug to other street drugs like heroin, cocaine, etc.

There's a **spirit of addiction** that keeps people enslaved to their particular substance or activity. This is NOT make-believe. There is a real demon assigned to keep you addicted. This adds to the difficulty of breaking the habit simply by willpower. You have both a physical and spiritual component keeping your addiction in place. The spiritual assignment

> There's a **spirit of addiction** that keeps people enslaved to their particular substance or activity. This is NOT make-believe. There is a real demon assigned to keep you addicted. This adds to the difficulty of breaking the habit simply by willpower. You have both a physical and spiritual component keeping your addiction in place.

behind all willful sin, including addictions, is to pervert the image of God in you, keeping you from walking out your true identity and destiny in Christ Jesus.

Because you have an agreement with the spirit of addiction, it is given access into your body through the gates involved with the addiction. For example, someone addicted to smoking has opened the taste gate, eye gate, smell gate, and touch gate (how the cigarette feels in their hand). Each of these parts of their physical body has felt pleasure from the addiction. The eye will associate seeing a cigarette with pleasure or a way to feel more relaxed, for example. In this way, the eye will pull the object toward you. See the Gates chapter for instructions on cleaning out and closing the gates. This needs to be done for all addictions.

STEPS TO FREEDOM

1. First, identify what emotions or beliefs caused you to take on the addiction. Do this by asking the following questions:

   What was happening at the time you started the addiction that caused you to feel you need that substance or activity? For example, were you feeling alone, abandoned, unloved, peer pressure to feel accepted, lost, not good enough, like I don't fit in?

   In one example, you may remember smoking in high school because it looked cool and all your friends were doing it. The next question would be, "How would it feel to NOT do what everybody else is doing?" In this case, you may feel like you wouldn't fit in and you might feel awkward or left out. Smoking brings a sense of belonging and camaraderie.

Write down your answer to the above question.

_____

_____

_____

_____

2. Determine whether this addiction could be generational by asking yourself, "Is there anyone in my family history who struggled with addictions?" If the answer is yes, then remember to include the generational component when saying the Value Exchange prayer.

3. The next step is to get an understanding of how your addiction is helping you cope with the feeling or belief statement above. You could also ask yourself, "How does this addiction (like smoking or eating) help me deal with the negative emotion I feel or believe?" For example, does this help me to escape, bring comfort, dull pain, relieve anxiety and feel more in control? Are you addicted to the adrenaline rush (of substances or risky activities like gambling,

Russian roulette, extreme and dangerous sports, etc.)? In the example from #1, you recognize that smoking helps you feel like you're accepted and belong.

4. Once you've identified the value of your addiction, you'll need to assess whether you're willing to let the addiction and its value go. Place your addiction before Jesus, asking yourself, "Am I willing to give this up?"

   a. Remember, you are allowing a demonic spirit to make sure your needs are met. Even though it feels so positive, you need Holy Spirit to expose the deception and give you truth! Ask Holy Spirit to show you what is truly happening in the spirit realm. What does the value of that addiction really look like?

   b. See Chapter 1 on Resistance if needed.

5. Once you're willing to break all agreements with the addiction and give up all its value, then do a Value Exchange.

6. Close the gates (see the Gates chapter).

7. Pray over your body and command the memory, habits, and all adverse effects of addiction on your body to go. Bless your body to come into alignment with the peace of Christ.

   Lord Jesus, I recognize that I've cursed my body by engaging in this addiction. I ask forgiveness for doing this. I choose to break this curse. I command all chemical imbalances occurring because of this addiction to come into balance with the peace of Christ. I break off all habits, cravings, and neurological pathways of addiction. I speak blessing over my body. Holy Spirit, I invite You to create new pathways that align themselves with Your perfect design.

8. Finally, go back into a memory to see if you still feel the emotion that caused you to engage in the addiction. Check each of your senses to make sure you don't feel any pull toward that substance or doing the activity.

You can find a free guide called "The 10 Signs You May Need a Value Exchange" on our website at **FreedomExpress16.org**.

EXAMPLES:

1. Gambling

If you have a gambling addiction, it could have come from an emotional wound or simply be an adrenaline rush and exhilaration that comes with winning or the possibility of winning. You may have felt powerless, so when you win a few times you begin to feel powerful, which urges you to try, try, and try again! Even after losing again and again, you still find yourself thrilled at the chance of winning, hoping for the big breakthrough. Giving that up would require giving up the rush, and the possibility of winning is over. That might feel like giving up hope. At some point, you may come to the end of yourself. Something will happen that brings you a realization that you are out of control and are losing everything because of it. That sometimes is enough to cause you to start seeking help.

If you had lack, then you could use gambling—even buying large quantities of lottery tickets—as your hope of getting out of the feeling of lack. At some point, you realize the destructive cycle of this addiction and want to be set free.

The prayer for gambling would be like the following:

Value Exchange:

Lord Jesus, I recognize I've taken on a spirit of addiction to gambling. I've used it to give me an emotional high, make me feel powerful, and give me hope for a breakthrough. I ask Your forgiveness for doing this. I choose to break my agreement with the spirit of addiction and its ungodly benefits. I command all demonic assignments connected to all these things to go now, in Jesus' name!

I also recognize that I have opened my eye, ear, and touch gates in an ungodly way. I ask Your forgiveness for doing this. I now chose to close all the gates I have opened. I command all demonic assignments that have passed through these gates to go out now, in Jesus' name! I command everything stolen from me through these gates to return to me now, in Jesus' name! Lord Jesus, I ask You to clean this out for me, fill it and seal me with what You have in exchange.

Be sure to take time to hear from the Lord.

Test your healing by going to a memory where you were feeling the strong need to gamble. Do you still feel pulled to do that? If you still feel the pull, then ask the Lord to show you why that pull is still there. What benefit have you missed? If you feel any resistance to completely letting this go, see the section in Chapter 1 on Dealing With Resistance.

2. Alcoholism

Over and over again you were rejected as a child and felt worthless. The repeated worthless feeling was very painful. You'll probably put guards up with other people for self-protection. You have this guard up, but it still hurts, so you need something additional to deal with the pain. You'll have to find a way to dull this pain, take it away, or find a way to take your mind off it. So, you drink enough alcohol to achieve the desired result. Drinking may be something you can control (when you feel out of control) or something you can hide ("because I can" and "nobody will know about it—so they can't stop me from doing it"). You may use alcohol to help you feel happy instead of sad. Or you could be an angry drinker, which feels more powerful. Or you could be a sad drinker, feeling a release through crying ("drowning your sorrows"). You may want to drink to lose your inhibitions, feel accepted by others, be able to act silly, and forget your insecurity. Strangely enough, alcohol helps you take down the very walls you put up for self-protection. A prayer for addiction to alcohol would be like the following:

Value Exchange:

Lord Jesus, I recognize I've taken on a spirit of addiction to alcohol. I have used this to dull pain/take pain away/take my mind off pain/to feel in control/to feel happy/to feel powerful/to release sadness/to feel accepted and take down my walls. I'm sorry and ask Your forgiveness for doing this. I now chose to break agreement with the spirit of addiction and give up all its ungodly benefits. I break off all demonic assignments connected to these things, in Jesus' name!

I also acknowledge that I have opened my mouth, eye, nose, and touch gates and given the demonic access through them. I ask Your forgivenss for doing this. I now choose to close all the gates I have opened. I command all demonic assignments that have passed through these gates to go out now (the way you came in), in Jesus' name! I command everything stolen from me through theses gates to return to me now, in Jesus' name! Lord Jesus, I ask You to clean this out for me, fill it, and give to me what You have in exchange.

Be sure to take time to receive from the Lord.

Remember to test your healing by going to a memory where you felt compelled to drink alcohol. Does it still feel true that you *need* to do that? If it feels calm and peaceful, then you've gotten a good exchange.

3. Pornography Addiction

You were exposed to pornography when you were around 12 years old by stumbling upon a website. Out of curiosity, you innocently took the bait, watching and then even fantasizing about being in the pictures or movie. In these fantasies, you felt powerful and desirable. You began to feel a heightened sense of value in these fantasies. You realize that fantasy has become an escape from real life problems and stresses. This way of escape is easy to keep a secret. That secret gives it more power because of feeling, "I got away with it." Secrecy stirs up the adrenaline (some people like to take chances and push the limits), which adds to the excitement.

Unlike other addictions, pornography especially appeals to the flesh. Every single sense gets "tickled" and your body wants to engage, so you begin masturbating. Pornography and fantasy are sexually arousing and appeal to the ears, eyes, and sexual organs. They open more gates than most other addictions. The gates you'll need to close depend on how far your addiction has progressed.

By using lust, the spirit of addiction motivates you to "get more" of that "good feeling," which can progress into watching more perverted pictures or movies (like child porn, bestiality, etc.) Eventually, fantasy tempts you to act out what you're seeing. The desires of lust are never satisfied, leaving you wanting more and more, progressing to higher levels of perversion and debasement. You realize that doing these things has negatively affected your relationships with people and with the Lord. You would like to be free from this.

Value Exchange:

Lord Jesus, I've taken on a spirit of addiction to pornography and masturbation. I've used this addiction to give me pleasure and value, and to feel more powerful. I recognize I have a spirit of lust motivating me to find more creative ways to get the things I desire. In doing this, I have opened my eye, ear, touch, mouth, nose, and sexual organ gates to the demonic and given them access into my body. I ask Your forgiveness for doing this. I now choose to break agreement with the spirit of addiction, masturbation, and lust. I choose to give up all their ungodly value. I break off all demonic assignments that have come against me and command them to go, in Jesus' name! I also choose to close all gates I have opened. I command all demonic assignments that have passed through these gates to go out now (the way you came in), in Jesus' name! I command everything stolen from me through these gates to return to me now, in Jesus' name! Lord Jesus, I ask You to clean all this out for me, seal it with what You have for me in exchange.

Be sure to take time to receive from the Lord.

Remember to test your healing by going to a memory where you felt compelled to watch pornography. Does it still feel true that you *need* to do that? If it feels calm and peaceful, then you've gotten a good exchange.

> **But I say to you that everyone who (so much as) looks at a woman with lust for her has already committed adultery with her in his heart.**
> ~*Matthew 5:28* (AMP)

4. Food Addiction

You've been trying to lose weight for a long time but just can't stick to a healthy meal plan consistently. To help understand what's behind your compulsion to eat too much, too often, or the wrong things, ask yourself these questions:

1. Am I using food for comfort? Food makes me feel better when I'm having a bad day or feeling sad.
2. Does eating help me feel in control? "It's the one thing I can control."
3. Do I eat because of boredom?
4. Do I always feel like I need something in my mouth (for comfort)?
5. Do I associate eating with feeling loved and accepted?
6. Do I see eating as a reward?
7. Is eating my "happy?" ☺
8. Do I want to be overweight so I'm not attractive to the opposite sex? Being unattractive protects me from being desirable, avoiding further abuse.
9. Does being overweight keep me from having to do things I don't want to do or to avoid situations that would draw attention to me?
10. Does being overweight feel like it keeps people from seeing the "real me"?

You may have multiple benefits contributing to your compulsion to eat.

Next, ask yourself how it would make you feel if you didn't have food to help you with those things. For instance, you may feel out of control or agitated. Once you identify how it made you feel, ask yourself if it would be okay to break agreement with the way food helps you stay in control or brings comfort. If it feels okay, then your Value Exchange would be like the below:

Value Exchange:

Lord Jesus, I recognize I've used food to _____ (bring comfort, help me feel in control, etc.), and I have come into agreement with a spirit of addiction. I ask Your forgiveness for doing this. I choose to break agreement with the spirit of addiction to food and to give up the benefits attached to it. I command all demonic assignments connected to this to go now, in Jesus' name!

I also recognize that I have opened my eye, nose, mouth, and touch gates and have given the demonic access into my body. I ask Your forgiveness for doing this. I now choose to close all the gates I have opened. I command all demonic assignments that have passed through these gates to go out now (the way you came in), in Jesus' name! I command everything stolen from me through these gates to return to me now, in Jesus' name!

Lord Jesus, I ask You to please clean this out for me, fill it and seal it with what You have in exchange.

Be sure to take time to receive from the Lord.

Remember to check a memory where you felt compelled to reach for food. Look at the benefits listed above and see if your belief statement still feels true. If those statements no longer feel true, then your next step is to close the gates by referring to Chapter 16. If any statement still feels true, then address the benefit again.

Prayer:

Refine my gaze, oh Lord. Fill me with longing for Your righteous ways. There are many roads I could take with many distractions along the way. Help me to stay on the straight and narrow!

Let your eyes look directly ahead (toward the path of moral courage). And let your gaze be fixed straight in front of you (toward the path of integrity).
~Proverbs 4:25 *(AMP)*

CHAPTER 15

BREAKING UNGODLY SOUL TIES

A soul tie is a connection or linking of two people in the spiritual realm. There are godly soul ties and ungodly soul ties. *Soul ties are a choice*—we choose which one to create. This choice is subconscious and happens naturally, for good or for bad. It's possible to create both in the same relationship. It is important to understand that breaking an ungodly soul tie will NOT break the godly one in healthy relationships.

A godly soul tie is created when the two people involved are acting in unity with the Lord's design in a healthy, balanced relationship. Godly soul ties are created for the purpose of bonding to another in love. For example, a godly soul tie exists in a *healthy* parent-child relationship as well as between a husband and wife in a *good* marriage. These kinds of soul ties are God-approved.

> **For this reason a man shall leave his father and his mother and shall be joined (and be faithfully devoted) to his wife, and the two shall become one flesh.**
> *~Ephesians 5:31* (AMP)

A healthy soul tie can also exist between two good friends. For example, Jonathon and David had a godly soul tie as described in the verse below:

**When David had finished speaking to Saul, the soul of
Jonathan was bonded to the soul of David,
and Jonathan loved him as himself.**
~1 Samuel 18:1 (AMP)

This kind of soul tie between friends is good because it's a bonding of healthy, godly love and the feelings and commitment that come with it.

In contrast, ungodly soul ties are a result of demonic knitting together of souls created outside of God's laws. For instance, an ungodly soul tie is created in the moment a person has sex outside of marriage or is involved in a homosexual relationship.

**Do you not know that the unrighteous will not inherit or
have any share in the Kingdom of God? Do not be deceived;
neither the sexually immoral, nor idolaters, nor adulterers,
nor effeminate (by perversion), nor those who participate in
homosexuality ... Do you not know that the one who joins
himself to a prostitute is one body *with her*? For He says,
"THE TWO SHALL BE ONE FLESH."**
~1 Corinthians 6:9, 16 (AMP)

Ungodly soul ties are also frequently created if there is strong physical, emotional, sexual, or spiritual abuse in a relationship. These ties are subconsciously developed to help cope in the relationship. Ungodly soul ties will keep us in bondage to another person. Even when there has been no contact for years there's an unexplainable pull involving feelings and memories connected to them. You may have trouble forgiving, or you may be holding bitterness and resentment, or wanting to bring justice even if you know that is not the Lord's heart for you. You can't "shake" them no matter how hard you try. Ungodly soul ties can also be created against your will, as in cases of rape and abuse. Demons and demonic assignments can be passed through these ties. As well, things can be stolen from you, like peace, joy, well-being, courage, etc.

EXAMPLES OF UNGODLY SOUL TIES INCLUDE THE FOLLOWING:

1. Sex outside of marriage including rape, adultery, homosexuality, and sexual abuse.

2. Protecting the "ideal" or fantasy of a love relationship by denying abuse.

3. Codependency: Controlling relationships (spiritual, verbal, physical abuse).

4. Codependency: Unhealthy, unbalanced "need to be needed"/neediness.

5. Elevating a person above God (someone you really love or admire more than God).

6. Unhealthy identification with someone else's emotional pain.

These ungodly ties may develop when you spend a lot of time with people. This tie is an "unhealthy emotional bond" linking or uniting yourself to another person.

Signs of an ungodly soul tie include the following:

1. Your mind is always pulled toward the other person. You keep thinking about them, even if you try not to. This can be tormenting. This ungodly soul tie keeps your mind "in bondage," wondering what the other person is doing and who they're with.

2. You rehearse times spent with the other person by replaying memories from the past (sometimes like a broken record).

3. You find yourself still grieving obsessively over a severed relationship with someone you once were close to.

4. Everything reminds you of the other person, leaving you confused and upset.

5. You feel anxious about losing the relationship with the other person because you can't live without them.

6. You might feel "addicted" to the other person, always wanting to be with them even though you know it is unreasonable, impossible, or even unsafe.

7. You need something from the other person to feel valued. Your well-being is dependent upon receiving their phone calls, texts, or spending time with them. Those unmet expectations will cause a confusing mix of anger and love.

8. You may feel depressed due to a constant intermingling of uneasiness (insecurity), anxiety, and sorrow. You may be disgusted by what you're doing (example: constantly checking their location or their Facebook page), yet powerless to stop doing it.

9. You might find yourself disobeying God because of the ungodly soul tie. For instance, you may continue to have sex outside of marriage, participate in drunken parties (something you wouldn't typically do, but you participate to please the other person), or pull away from God and your church family, etc. This will distract you from doing your best for the Lord, keeping you from walking out His higher call in your life.

10. You may *feel controlled* by the other person and find yourself trying to please them, hoping to avoid their anger. You may avoid confronting them about their issues (like addictions or emotional problems, for example) out of fear, enabling their bad behaviors in your pursuit of keeping them happy.

11. You may find yourself submitting to their expectations of you (being controlled by them), hoping to earn value and love.

If you found yourself relating to some of the above examples, you may unknowingly have taken on an ungodly soul tie with another person. But your situation is not hopeless!

Jesus made the payment for your freedom and wants to help you!

In the following paragraphs, you'll find examples of common ungodly soul ties and Value Exchange prayers that will set you free! In each example, you will want to ask yourself, prior to doing the exchange, whether you have any resistance to breaking the ungodly soul tie. Remember, the Lord will not go against your will. So, if you really don't want to give it up, He will not remove it. You'll need to address the resistance with Him before saying the prayer. Go to the end of Chapter 1 to address resistance.

EXAMPLES:

1. **Sex outside of marriage, adultery, homosexuality, and sexual abuse**

   You find yourself in a serious relationship. You have sex a couple times. You realize that when you're not with your partner, you're constantly thinking about them. Using your phone, you're always checking their location, worrying that they could be with someone else. You text them to get reassurance but get hurt and offended when they don't answer back right away. You get disgusted with yourself for being so needy but can't stop. Eventually you spiral into a depression and are angry much of the time because of insecurity (or fear of abandonment). Upon reading this manual, you realize you're caught in this cycle and need to break off the ungodly soul tie.

   Value Exchange:

   Lord Jesus, I recognize I've created an ungodly soul tie with my significant other. I'm sorry and ask Your forgiveness for doing this. I choose to forgive them and myself for creating this ungodly soul tie. I recognize that I'm using this soul tie to try to feel safe, connected, and loved. I now choose to break agreement with this ungodly soul tie and all the ungodly ways I've used it. I command every ungodly thing deposited in me to go out now, in Jesus' name! I command that everything stolen from me must return to me now, in Jesus' name! Lord Jesus, I ask You to clean this out for me and fill my soul with what You value in exchange.

   Be sure to take time to receive from the Lord.

Remember to put yourself in a memory where you felt insecure, needing to check on their whereabouts. Do you still feel pulled to engage in that behavior? Are you still needing reassurance? Are you still offended when they didn't text back right away? Is the memory peaceful? If not, then address the negative emotion or belief still present and do another Value Exchange.

2. **Protecting the "ideal" of a love relationship by denying abuse**

This happens by not holding someone you love accountable for their abusive behavior in order to preserve the "love bond."

For example, a child is physically and emotionally abused by their parent. They love their parent and can't make sense of the abuse because they've done everything they can to be lovable. There is no other explanation for the abuse, except they must be the problem and deserve the abuse. It can't be the parent's fault. It must be their fault; they weren't "good enough" and may have been told it was their fault. In this way, the child believes they deserved it.

By believing they deserved abusive treatment, the child protects themself from being mad at their parent and having to admit the parent did not love them well. Admitting the parent's behavior was wrong would feel like betrayal and might destroy what little relationship they still have with each other. Therefore, the child denies the parent was wrong in the abuse, accepting "blame" to explain why they acted that way. "It's better to blame myself" than to feel unloved. When you get an understanding of the ungodly tie created between you and your parent/abuser, this is how to break it:

Value Exchange:

Lord Jesus, I recognize I've created an ungodly soul tie with (my abuser) _____. I've used this soul tie to protect my "ideal" of the love bond that I desired. I also have used this soul tie to protect me from being angry with this person. I ask forgiveness for doing this. I choose to forgive them and myself for creating this ungodly tie. I choose to break agreement with the lie that it was my fault/I deserved it. I choose to break this soul tie and give up all its ungodly benefits. I command all demonic assignments connected to this to go, in Jesus' name! I command that every ungodly thing deposited in me must go now, in Jesus' name! I command that everything stolen from me must return to me now, in Jesus' name! Lord Jesus, I ask that You cleanse this place and fill me with Your truth.

Be sure to take time to receive from the Lord.

Remember to check a memory where you KNOW you felt it was your fault. Listen to the abusive words spoken to you and see how it feels. Does it still feel true that you are the problem? If it's all clear, then you've gotten a good exchange! If not, address whatever feelings are left in the memory with another Value Exchange.

3. **Codependency – Controlling relationships (spiritual, verbal, physical abuse)**

This typically occurs in unbalanced relationships in which one person is dysfunctional and the other person becomes that way by trying to keep the dysfunctional person satisfied. There's a "demanding/controlling" person and a "self-sacrificing" person. The dominating person often gets angry if their needs are not met.

They may have addictions (like alcoholism) that they need in order to feel calm and peaceful. The spouse may have to walk on eggshells to avoid triggering them. Supplying them with alcohol helps keep the peace. In doing this, the "self-sacrificing" person is enabling their spouse's behavior.

The dominating person may use manipulation to control their partner. As a result, there is serious dysfunction in the relationship, creating a never-ending cycle of brokenness.

Example: Several years after getting married, you recognize that your spouse is becoming more easily irritated and sometimes angry about some of your choices. Their disapproval and/or anger causes you to feel hurt (unloved and rejected), anxious, and controlled. When you've done something that could make them unhappy, you get scared about how they'll respond. You sometimes find yourself "walking on eggshells" around them to avoid conflict. Even when they're being nice, you still *feel* controlled. You start making decisions about what to do, or not do, based upon what you feel would make your spouse upset or not. You start to feel like you must get permission for everything you do.

You recognize the dysfunction in your relationship is coming from trying to protect yourself. You're willing to give up the value and pray the following:

Value Exchange:

Lord Jesus, I recognize I've become codependent with my spouse. In doing this, I've created an ungodly soul tie with them. I've used this soul tie to protect myself and keep the peace. I ask Your forgiveness for doing this and I choose to forgive them and myself for creating it. I now choose to break this ungodly soul tie. I command that every ungodly thing deposited in me through this soul tie must go out now, in Jesus' name! I command that everything stolen from me must return to me now, in Jesus' name! Lord Jesus, I ask You to clean this all out and give me what You value in exchange.

Be sure to take time to receive from the Lord.

Check a memory to see if you still feel controlled, unloved/rejected, and anxious. If everything is peaceful, you've gotten a perfect Value Exchange. If not, then identify what emotion/beliefs are still uncomfortable and do another exchange until all is at peace.

4. **Codependency – Unhealthy, unbalanced "need to be needed"/ neediness**

Example: Marsha is a very compassionate person who loves to help people. She has a big heart and is very sensitive to the emotional needs of others. Marsha found out that her cousin Ashley's husband committed suicide. This was a total shock to Ashley since she thought they had a happy, loving marriage. Ashley started to blame herself and went into a deep depression. She found it hard to take care of the household and meet the needs of her children. Marsha began to spend a lot of time with Ashley trying to help her with physical needs as well as emotional support. Ashley became dependent on Marsha's attention and care. This knitted the two cousins in an unhealthy bond of codependency. Marsha needed to be "needed." They met each other's "neediness."

A Value Exchange for Marsha or Ashley would look like the following:

Lord Jesus, I recognize that I've created an ungodly soul tie with _____. I've used this soul tie to feel needed (Marsha). I've used this soul tie to feel taken care of and more secure (Ashley). I ask forgiveness for doing this. I choose now to break agreement with this soul tie and the ways I've used it to cope. I break off all demonic assignments connected to this ungodly soul tie and command them to go, in Jesus' name! I command every ungodly thing that has come to me through this soul tie to go now, in Jesus' name. I command that everything stolen from me must return to me now, in Jesus' name! Jesus, I ask You to clean this place out and fill me with Your truth.

Be sure to take time to receive from the Lord.

5. **Elevating another person above the Lord**

This occurs when a person is more important to you than God. Signs that you've done this include the following: you think about them constantly, you always want to be with them and talk to them. You figure out ways to get them to pay attention to you. You may panic when you don't hear from them. In this way, you place demands on that person to be responsible for your well-being. This person can take the place of Holy Spirit in your life. This can also involve fantasizing about the other person in the role you feel is missing in your life—like a mother, spouse, friend, or child.

If you have elevated another person above the Lord, a Value Exchange would look like the following:

Lord Jesus, I confess that I've created an ungodly soul tie with _____. In doing this, I have elevated them above You. I've placed the responsibility for my well-being on them. I ask Your forgiveness for doing this. I choose to break this soul tie. I take the responsibility for my well-being out of their hands. I release them from that responsibility. I choose to put the responsibility back into Your hands, Jesus, where it belongs. I command every ungodly thing that has come to me through this soul tie to leave now in Jesus' name. I command that everything stolen from me through this soul tie must return to me now, in the name of Jesus! Lord Jesus, I ask You to clean this place out and fill me with what You have in exchange.

Be sure to take time to receive from the Lord.

Remember to look at your relationship with your friend—how do you see them now, in comparison to the Lord? Do you have a right perspective of their importance in your life? If your perspective has changed and the Lord takes first place, then you had a good Value Exchange. If not, then identify the emotions/beliefs and the coping mechanisms that are still causing imbalance and do another Value Exchange.

6. Unhealthy identification with someone else's emotional pain

This type of soul tie can happen when a person becomes sympathetic of someone else's emotional distress and literally chooses to "take on" the other person's emotional state as their own. Doing this brings an emotional connection with them, because you truly can identify with their pain. You might even feel like you're helping to take some pain away from them by carrying it yourself. Or you may take on their pain to show sympathy, proving you care.

Example: You have witnessed your child being hurt in ways that are painful to watch. There's nothing you can do to change their situation. And you can't take their pain away. You start to identify with their emotional pain. This could make you feel closer to your child, since you're sharing their sadness and suffering. Worrying about their emotional well-being could motivate you to find ways to make them happy again. You may be overly protective of them because you understand their pain. In some cases, your child may act out in unhealthy ways, and you defend their actions because you don't want them to be judged and feel more emotional pain.

If you feel like you have this type of ungodly soul tie, you would pray like the following:

Value Exchange:

Lord Jesus, I recognize I've created an ungodly soul tie with my child. I have used this soul tie to have a closer bond with my child. I've used it to motivate myself to make them happy, taking responsibility for their well-being. I ask forgiveness for creating this ungodly soul tie. I choose now to break this soul tie. I command every ungodly thing that has come to me through this tie to go out now, in Jesus' name. I command that everything stolen from me must return to me now, in Jesus' name. Jesus, would You please clean this place out and give me what You value in exchange.

Be sure to take time to receive from the Lord.

Remember to check a memory after each exchange.

Check a memory where you know this soul tie would have existed. How does this memory feel to you now? If you have complete peace, then you've gotten a good exchange. If not, check to see what negative emotion/belief is still present and do a Value Exchange for it.

BREAKING THE RESISTANCE:

Sometimes a person will hesitate breaking an ungodly soul tie. The thought of breaking the soul tie feels like it would be betraying or breaking the love connection with the other person in some way. The soul tie may keep fantasy in place and sometimes that seems better than reality.

> Breaking an ungodly soul tie will ONLY REMOVE THE UNGODLY aspect of the relationship. It will leave all godly parts in place.

It is important to understand that breaking an ungodly soul tie will NOT break the godly one in place with healthy relationships. If you feel resistance letting this soul tie go during the prayer of breaking it, you need to address the reason behind the resistance. There are subconscious benefits to having these ungodly soul ties.

For example, you could fear letting go of the soul tie created from committing adultery because you would no longer have the fantasy to make you feel more desirable and loved. The reasons could be many.

In this case, ask yourself, "What am I afraid of losing?" You might respond by saying, "I won't feel desirable anymore." Then ask yourself if you would be willing to let Jesus give you His perspective about that belief. If so, just say, "Lord Jesus, I give You permission to share Your thoughts with me about this belief that breaking this soul tie will make me feel less desirable and unloved." Have the expectation that Jesus will share His perspective with you somehow. He knows how to respond in a way you'll be able to receive. Once you receive from Him, any resistance is usually broken.

If you haven't already repented for committing adultery, now would be a good time. Also ask yourself if you can forgive yourself for doing this.

Frequently people hesitate to break an ungodly soul tie, believing they'll lose the relationship or there won't be a godly tie left. Bear in mind that breaking an ungodly soul tie will ONLY REMOVE THE UNGODLY aspect of the relationship. It will leave all godly parts in place. If you feel resistance to breaking an unhealthy soul tie, then ask the Lord for His perspective of this belief. Breaking the ungodly soul tie ONLY breaks the ungodly soul tie, but sometimes people need to be convinced by the Lord.

> **Beyond all these things put on and wrap yourselves in (unselfish) love, which is the perfect bond of unity (for everything is bound together in agreement when each one seeks the best for others). Let the peace of Christ (the inner calm of one who walks daily with Him) be the controlling factor in your hearts (deciding and settling questions that arise). To this peace indeed you were called as members in one body (of believers). And be thankful (to God always).**
> *~Colossians 3:14 (AMP)*

Prayer:

Papa, thank You that the passion of a warrior is being matured in me! Cause me to stand in the "knowing" of the authority of Christ that I've been given. Open my eyes to see the power of the "love bond" I have with You! The covenant love that nothing has the power to break!

CHAPTER 16

THE PHYSICAL GATES

There are spiritual laws operating in our world that have been established by God. Every being that exists must abide by them. The worldview does not have a legal right to change God's laws. We may or may not agree with them, but the spiritual realm will always be bound to them. There's a consequence for disobeying His laws. With our free will, we either open a door to the Light of Christ (through Holy Spirit) or to the darkness of the demonic.

> The worldview does not have a legal right to change God's laws. We may or may not agree with them, but the spiritual realm will always be bound to them.

Our bodies are meant to be a holy habitation for Holy Spirit. We are truly a house of the Lord! All our five physical senses are a gateway to the physical and spiritual realm. Disobedience or sin causes a misuse of these gates and has potential to open a door to the demonic. Gates are opened due to physical exposure to something ungodly. This can be willful sin, unintentional sin, or ungodly acts forced upon you.

For example, many people use cigarettes to calm themselves when they're feeling anxious. When this happens, their mind will associate smoking with stress relief. Any time they start feeling anxious again, the brain will want to default to smoking another cigarette to achieve the desired effect. In this way, they've attached a positive benefit (of comfort) to a negative thing (smoking, along with its side effects of causing disease) and have involved three physical senses. The senses involved include touch (holding the cigarette in their hand and mouth), sight, and taste. After breaking agreement with the addiction to smoking, all physical gates involved will need to be cleaned out and closed.

> **Therefore I urge you, brothers and sisters, by the mercies of God, to present your bodies (dedicating all of yourselves, set apart) as a living sacrifice, holy and well-pleasing to God, which is your rational (logical, intelligent) act of worship.**
> ~*Romans 12:1* *(AMP)*

EXAMPLES OF THE PHYSICAL GATES:

1. **Eye/vision**:

   The eye sends visual images directly to the brain. Your brain next determines how to think and what to believe about those images. Your mind may reject what you saw. Or you may be tempted and curious about the image and choose to pursue more information about it. You may feel your body responding to the picture, causing you to want to look more. The images we choose to look at will remain in our memory banks. Those images, for good or for bad, will produce fruit after their kind. Without mind renewal, bad images have the potential to grow, like a weed.

The eye is the lamp of your body. When your eye is clear (spiritually perceptive, focused on God), your whole body also is full of light (benefiting from God's precepts). But when it is bad (spiritually blind), your body also is full of darkness (devoid of God's word). Be careful, therefore, that the light that is in you is not darkness. So if your whole body is illuminated, with no dark part, it will be entirely bright (with light), as when the lamp gives you light with its bright rays."
~Luke 11:34-36 (AMP)

2. Mouth/taste or sensation

Our tongue is a sensory tool that can be used for good or bad sensory experiences. This sense of taste adds to any oral experience, for either good or bad. Possible negative examples involving taste include the use of tobacco, alcohol, and addiction to food. Taste may also be involved with sexual experiences or participation in dark rituals where you must drink/eat something ungodly, for example. From that moment on, you will associate the taste with the emotions you were experiencing at the time of use.

The mouth is also an opening that allows substances to get access into your body. Those substances may not have a taste. But the feeling in your mouth brings an emotional response and expectation of the effect that particular substance will have on your body and mind. For instance, a narcotic pill does not have a taste, but your mind will associate the action of swallowing a pill with the desired outcome.

For the heavy drinker and the glutton will come to poverty, and the drowsiness (of overindulgence) will clothe one with rags.
~Proverbs 23:21 (AMP)

3. Ear/hearing

Sounds are received into the mind through our ears. These include spoken words, music, and sounds of nature. EVERYTHING that makes noise travels into our mind. We will interpret these sounds by what we choose to think in the moment, resulting in a holy or unholy response. The enemy gets into our minds through what we listen to. We can become desensitized to ungodly music and words. We may even find ourselves singing words to songs that glorify anger, violence, objectifying women, drugs, sex, or involve profanity, not really paying attention to what's being spoken. Have you ever caught yourself singing a song and suddenly realize what you're really singing?! And you're appalled. If you listen to cuss words enough, you won't even notice when people cuss, and may find yourself using those words yourself.

What the ear hears may even elicit a sexual physical response. Dark music can also draw someone into self-harm, suicide, or even murder.

For example, people connect to music at an emotional level, relating to feelings expressed in the tone of the melody and its words. Music can take your bad feelings away, like a drug. It could also distract you from thinking about your problems. Music is the universal language of emotion, speaking louder than words and expressing what you're feeling and can't put into your own words. Slow tempos may cause sadness whereas music that's upbeat makes you feel courageous and happy. Someone depressed may find comfort listening to depressing music.

For the time will come when people will not tolerate sound doctrine and accurate instruction (that challenges them with God's truth); but wanting to have their ears tickled (with something pleasing), they will accumulate for themselves (many) teachers (one after another, chosen) to satisfy their own desires and to support the errors they hold, and will turn their ears away from the truth and will wander off into myths and man-made fictions (and will accept the unacceptable).
~2 Timothy 4:2-4 (AMP)

4. Touch

Our skin receives sensory input that may be pleasurable, painful, or uncomfortable and sends them to the brain for interpretation. Our brain will then determine how to respond to those sensations. As a result, our brain stores the touch information, associating it with good or bad memories. For example, your body will remember when a person comes up behind you, putting their arms around you in a hug, then proceeds to sexually abuse you. Years later, when your spouse comes from behind to give you a hug, you might feel immediately fearful because of the prior abuse. Your brain and body react to the hug from your spouse as a "bad" thing, even when done in love.

Another example is the pleasure of holding something you really enjoy, like cigarettes, stuffed animals, blankets, worry rocks, talisman (an object felt to have magical/spiritual power), or other objects. We displace Holy Spirit when we become dependent on an object to help us feel safe, comforted, or in control. In doing this, our well-being is dependent upon holding or touching that object.

> **"…except the fruit from the tree which is in the middle of the garden. God said, 'You shall not eat from it nor *touch* it, otherwise you will die.'"**
> ~*Genesis 3:3* (AMP)

5. Nose/smell

The nose receives odors or scents from everything that has one! Our minds are quick to receive this information and determine a course of action. We're drawn to things that smell good and are repelled by those that are offensive. The sense of smell draws us into or away from an experience, for good or for bad.

For instance, a child abused by a family member in a basement of their house will remember that smell. As an adult, they may have flashbacks every time they smell that familiar basement odor/scent—no matter what setting they're in.

In another example, the brain of a person who is addicted to cigarettes or marijuana will attach pleasure to their smell. They may really want to quit smoking, but every time they smell those odors, they associate the smell with pleasure and are drawn to it again.

> **No temptation (regardless of its source) has overtaken or enticed you that is not common to human experience (nor is any temptation unusual or beyond human resistance); but God is faithful (to His word-He is compassionate and trustworthy), and He will not let you be tempted beyond your ability (to resist), but along with the temptation He (has in the past and is now and) will (always) provide the way out as well, so that you will be able to endure it (without yielding, and will overcome temptation with joy).**
> *~1 Corinthians 10:13* (AMP)

6. Sexual organs

Our sexual organs are intended by God for mutual bonding, pleasure, and procreation. However, any use outside of their original blessed design is an open door for all manner of ungodly perversion. This is enhanced because sex is one gate that has the potential to open up the gates to the other five physical senses!

For example, watching pornography engages physical sensations that are pleasurable. This can lead to addiction, which progresses to an insatiable desire for more. This causes you to search for more inventive ways to involve touch as you watch porn. You now may want to engage in ungodly acts with your partner, hoping to increase the physical stimulation by acting out what you've seen. This breaks down the moral standards set by God for the proper use of sexual engagement.

Fantasy is strongly connected to pornography, which tries to satisfy areas of lack in your heart. Using fantasy, you can enhance sexual acts in your mind, becoming convinced the other person is respecting, loving, accepting, desiring you, etc. Whatever you believe you're lacking in real life, *you can be* in this fantasy world. For example, you feel like you're bringing another person sexual satisfaction that nobody else can.

Lust is a natural result of watching pornography and fantasizing. Lust is an insatiable desire for sexual stimulation for self-pleasure alone. It does not regard the other person involved. They become an object of your pleasure.

Pornography coupled with masturbation is also used as a strong emotional release and exhilaration that easily overrides any emotional stress you were feeling previously.

As with all sin, sexual sins can get very dark and perverted. And that is the enemy's goal.

> **Run away from sexual immorality (in any form, whether thought or behavior, whether visual or written). Every other sin that a man commits is outside the body, but the one who is sexually immoral sins against his own body.**
> ~1 Corinthians 6:18 (AMP)

7. Spiritual vision (third eye)

Spiritual vision connects us to the spiritual realm. It is a physical part of our brain (the pineal gland and forehead region) some scientists believe acts like an antenna, receiving and interpreting spiritual information, then sending it to one or more of the five physical senses and soul. This information increases our understanding and may cause an emotional response. Throughout history, people have believed the Spiritual Eye is the doorway or gateway into greater spiritual enlightenment. In New Age, it is called the Third Eye (Chakra).

Our spiritual "eye" (antenna) needs to be opened. But as a Christian, this opening needs to occur by the power of Holy Spirit. In this way, our spiritual awareness is sanctified and set apart for God only. The safe way to open your spiritual senses is through meditating on the Scriptures, worship, prayer, and mind renewal. Mind renewal works by removing everything that hinders the relationship between you and God. As you learn to communicate with Holy Spirit, the spiritual eye is opened more and more.

The spiritual eye can be opened illegally by chanting, meditation, sun gazing, drugs, mushrooms, etc. You might inherit an ungodly opening of the spiritual eye. For example, you may feel (or tap into) another person's emotions or thoughts, not realizing that not everybody can. The problem with feeling other people's emotions is that you may judge them, determine your truth by what they're feeling, or act and react from what you feel coming from them rather than relying on the wisdom and truth of God.

An opened spiritual eye may allow you to see (in your mind's eye or literally) angels, demons, colors, symbols of emotions or woundedness, and things of this nature. You may smell scents or odors originating from the spirit realm. The smell of sulfur is demonic. You may taste something, sweet or bitter, depending on what is present in the spirit realm. The ungodly use of this spiritual sensing may help you engage with a "spirit guide" to help bring healing, guidance, foretelling futures for people, etc.

BELOW ARE EXAMPLES OF HOW THE PHYSICAL GATES GET OPENED:

1. **TV/movies/music/phone/computer screens/books/magazines**

   Examples include pornography, dark rap/music (like about suicide/violence), watching cartoons in which something evil appears acceptable and even friendly.

2. **Use of recreational drugs/abuse of prescription drugs**

   Examples include pain meds, ADD/ADHD meds, anxiety meds, sleeping pills or mixtures of the above).

3. **Perversion**

   Examples include sexual behavior or desire considered abnormal or unacceptable, such as homosexuality, pedophilia, sadistic sex, orgies or bestiality) or perverted acts done against your will.

4. **The occult/satanism/rituals/secret societies/witchcraft/ participation in chants/seances, playing with Ouija boards, tarot cards, psychic readings, horoscopes**

5. **False religions/cults**

6. **Trauma/abuse - physical, emotional, sexual (molestation or rape)**

7. **Addictions**

8. **Ungodly soul tie**

   Any sexual contact outside of heterosexual marriage including vaginal sex, anal intercourse, oral sex, fingering/hand jobs, etc.

> **And not a creature exists that is concealed from His sight, but all things are open and exposed, and revealed to the eyes of Him with whom we have to give account.**
> *~Hebrews 4:13* (AMP)

If you identified some gates that need to be closed from the list above, you must first determine how you used each open gate to benefit you. Ask yourself questions like, "How does this make me feel to participate in the activity associated with the gate?" "What's drawing me to doing the activity above?" "What would I feel if I didn't do the activity connected to the gate?"

1. What benefits do you get from the above activity? (Example: comfort, power, joy, etc.)

2. Identify the feeling or belief by asking, "How would it make me feel not to have that benefit?"

3. Is the activity you're doing generational? If so, that will need to be added to your Value Exchange prayer.

4. Are you willing to give up all benefits and close the gate?

5. If so, then proceed with a Value Exchange.

6. If not, then deal with the resistance. Ask yourself if you're willing to ask the Lord for His perspective of your benefit. You may also refer to the end of Chapter 1 for help.

EXAMPLES:

1. Substance Abuse

You just finished doing a Value Exchange in the Addictions chapter. Now it's time to close the gates! Start by determining what gates were opened by using the substance or engaging in the activity. For example, smoking would open the mouth (taste), touch (the feeling of holding the cigarette), and nose (the smell gives pleasure) gates.

A Value Exchange would be like this:

Lord Jesus, I recognize that I've opened my mouth, touch, and nose gates and have given the demonic spirit of addiction access into my body. I am sorry and ask Your forgiveness for doing this. I now choose to break agreement with the spirit of addiction and close my mouth, touch, and nose gates. I give up all the ungodly value that I placed on them. I now command that every ungodly thing deposited in me through these gates must go out now the way it came in! I command everything stolen from me to be returned to me now in Jesus' name! I break this habit off my body! I command all chemical dependencies connected to this addiction to be broken now! I bless my body to come into perfect alignment with the perfect peace of Christ. Lord Jesus, I ask You to please clean, seal, and fill this place with what You have in exchange.

Be sure to take time to receive from the Lord.

Go back into a memory where you felt the need to engage in the addiction and see if it still feels true that you need to do these things. What revelations do you have in the memory now?

2. **Fantasy about a homosexual relationship**

The culture has embraced homosexuality and being bisexual as the "norm." Despite your Christian upbringing, you start to believe that there is really nothing wrong with that belief. You feel alone and joining such a close-knit group of other people seems like a fun way to feel loved and accepted. As a result, you find yourself fantasizing about engaging in this kind of relationship. One weekend at a convention with your church, you saw people your age giving their lives to Jesus, going to the altar in tears, and confessing their sins. You were suddenly convicted about your thought life. Now you would like to be free from these fantasies.

Value Exchange:

Lord Jesus, I recognize that I've opened my ear and eye gates and started to fantasize about having an ungodly, homosexual relationship in order to feel loved and accepted instead of feeling alone. I'm sorry and ask Your forgiveness for doing this. I now choose to break agreement with homosexuality and fantasy connected to it and give up their comfort, acceptance, and love. I choose to close my eye and ear gates. I command all demonic assignments connected to these things to go, in Jesus' name! I command everything deposited in me through these gates to go out, the way you came in, in Jesus' name. I command everything stolen from me through these gates must return to me now, in Jesus' name! Lord Jesus, I ask that You please clean this all out for me and give me what You have in exchange.

Be sure to take time to hear from the Lord.

Remember to check a memory connected to the fantasy and see how it feels. If it's all clear and peaceful, then you have gotten a good exchange. If not, then address any remaining beliefs or emotions in the memory.

If you feel resistance, then go to the section in Chapter 1 on Dealing With Resistance.

3. **Feeling the emotions of others (ungodly use)**

Growing up, you naturally tuned in to the emotions of others and subconsciously used this information to know how to act around people. This kept you safe and helped you earn favor. You didn't realize you were doing this. However, as an adult, you realized you could tell, by *feeling*, if someone was having a good or bad day, even before they spoke. You felt their "warmth" or "coolness" and responded appropriately. As you matured, you've grown in skill with using this emotional information. Eventually, have emotions started to "trip you up" when you take people's negative emotions personally, believing it's directed toward you. You also find yourself feeling anxious after being around other another anxious person. Emotions feel very intense, and you often get overtaken by them. After talking to your spiritual mentor about this, you realize that feeling people's emotions was inherited (generational). Access to other people's emotions involved opening your spiritual eye in a way that was "illegal" because it was opened for self-protection and to know how to think and act around people. In doing this, you can "read their mail" without their consent. The emotions detected from others relay information to you about them, which is translated into a message that *feels true*. In this way, the message received from emotion becomes "truth" to you. You hadn't realized that *emotion speaks*. Your mentor helps you to understand that by agreeing with the message from emotion, you're not even hearing the Lord's truth and you are "emotionally driven." You're not using wisdom or discernment. You have displaced Holy Spirit as your source of truth. Uggghhhhh!!!!!!!!!

The Value Exchange would look something like this:

Lord Jesus, I recognize that I've received a generational curse of an illegally opened spiritual eye gate. I've used this to feel the emotions of others so I know how to navigate around them to keep me safe and to gain people's approval. I've also allowed emotion to determine my truth rather than the Truth. I ask forgiveness for doing this. I choose now to break this generational curse and the illegal opening of my spiritual eye gate and all the ungodly ways I've used it. I break agreement with the belief that emotion has the power to determine Truth. I command all demonic assignments connected to this curse and beliefs to go now, in Jesus' name! I now close the spiritual eye gate. I command every ungodly thing that passed to me through this gate to go out the way you came in, in Jesus' name! I command everything stolen from me through this gate to return to me now, in Jesus' name! Lord Jesus, I ask that You clean this out and seal this gate with your Truth.

Be sure to take time to receive from the Lord.

Check a memory where you know you were using feelings to navigate a situation. Does it still feel true that feelings determine truth? What truth are you receiving there now?

4. **Childhood friend**

You felt alone and neglected as a child. You had a favorite cartoon that had little witches and other types of creatures who were casting spells and doing magic. You got one of the stuffed toys for Christmas from that cartoon. Because of your loneliness, you started talking to this little creature. Eventually, you felt like the creature was talking back to you and you began to have conversations. It told you that it would be your friend and protect you so you'll never have to be lonely again. As you grew up, you eventually realized you had this voice in your head always wanting to keep you safe, comfort you, and give advice. As an adult, you realize this voice was not helpful, and kept you isolated and fearful. You realize this voice is not from the Lord and you need to get rid of it.

The Value Exchange would look something like this:

Lord Jesus, I recognize that I've felt alone and neglected, and have accepted an ungodly childhood "friend." I recognize this friend is a demonic voice and I've used this to give myself advice, comfort, and protection. I also recognize I opened my eye and ear (hearing) gates to the demonic and gave them access. I ask forgiveness for doing this. I choose to break agreement with this ungodly childhood "friend" and its ungodly benefits. I command all demonic assignments connected to it to go, in Jesus' name! I command everything that came in through my eye/ear gate must go out now, the way you came in, in Jesus' name. I command everything stolen through my eye/ear gates to be returned now, in Jesus' name. Lord Jesus, I ask that You clean these places out and give me what You value in exchange.

Take time to receive from the Lord.

Remember to check a memory where you leaned on this voice for support. Also check to see if you still feel alone or neglected. If the memory feels clear, then you have gotten a good Value Exchange. If not, then see what still feels uncomfortable and address that with a Value Exchange.

Prayer:

Holy, Holy are You, oh God, Lord most high! I exalt You with the highest praise for You alone are worthy—worthy to be praised! Righteous are Your ways, oh Lord. How I adore You! Open my eyes, Lord, to see more of You. Your mighty works are a display of Your goodness. Give me eyes to see the depth of Your love, oh God. Open the eyes of my heart to see the expanse of Yours. Your love draws me into a depth of relationship that leaves me breathless. My heart is full of You, oh Lord, and all I want is more, for only You can satisfy. Oh, how sweet is that!

Chapter 17

THE SHEPHERD

As I (Londa Harwell) was sitting pondering what relationship with Jesus looks like, I began to see this picture in my mind play out. I found myself lying down in a field of beautiful, fragrant flowers. The flowers radiated with color, aroma, and God's light. It was so very peaceful, feeling the cool grass beneath me and the tickle of the flowers around me. The sunshine was caressing me with its warmth that felt so healing, restoring my energy and well-being. Suddenly I heard the flowers sort of whispering in a hushed tone filled with awe. I opened my eyes and there stood the Lord Jesus as my shepherd! He had the biggest warm smile and His eyes were dancing with delight—a delight to be with me! He then reached down and stretched out His hand, and as I took it, He lifted me up to my feet. Isn't that just like Him? We began to walk; He never let go of my hand. His staff was in His other hand. It looked ancient and well-used but strong and efficient at the same time. I knew that many people had been snatched from the clutches of the enemy with its wonderful, hooked end. My attention went to His hand. I knew the scar would be there. I've seen it before, many times, and it always humbles me to the core. I know my sin put that nail in His hand, but I also know His amazing forgiveness. I love holding His hand and I love feeling the scar. It is undeniable proof of His love for me! His hands are warm and have a gentleness that seems contradictory of the confident strength I feel in them—a strength that can steady me in any situation where I find myself unsure of my footing! His clothing is that of a humble shepherd.

As we begin walking, I realize we are leaving the meadow. Now I find we are walking on a narrow path that leads up the side of a tall mountain. At first, the path is lovely with the song of birds and a few flowers and only a few small rocks on the path that I can easily kick out of the way. We cross a little stream happily going its way and only a couple of the steppingstones are a bit slippery. I am full of confidence and joy to be with my friend Jesus! As we climb, I notice how the green foliage is leaving us and the songbirds are getting scarce. Also, the path narrows and the rocks in the way become gradually bigger. I also see that the mountain is very tall and the drop-off is becoming progressively steeper and I become more and more aware of my frailty. Jesus still has my hand but I find I am becoming more and more distracted by the increasing dangers. Now we are seeing an occasional wild beast, like a bear or mountain lion that standing on the path and challenging our right to go farther! Then a rattlesnake or a scorpion is trying to get my feet! Sometimes when I take a step, the path collapses and I lose my footing! In each case, fear rises in my heart as I gaze upon the challenge blocking my progress. My thoughts are overtaken with negative beliefs about my abilities or wrong thinking about Jesus' intentions for leading me to this path. But I have found my Jesus to be a faithful shepherd. He never once lets go of my hand, even as the challenges became harder and seemingly more threatening. As I learn to trust Him to never let go I begin to confess every struggle of my heart to Him. And as I learn to listen to His heart for me, His intentions become clear as my gaze shifts away from the challenge, and I fix my eyes on Him; doubts flee and confidence in His faithfulness to love me well rises up within me! Suddenly I find we are on top of the mountain and it was actually flat ground all along! It is truly a matter of perspective!

The Lord is my Shepherd [to feed, to guide and to shield me], I shall not want. He lets me lie down in green pastures; He leads me beside the still and quiet waters. He refreshes and restores my soul (life); He leads me in the paths of righteousness for His name's sake. Even though I walk through the [sunless] valley of the shadow of death, I fear no evil, for You are with me; Your rod [to protect] and Your staff [to guide], they comfort and console me. You prepare a table before me in the presence of my enemies. You have anointed and refreshed my head with oil; My cup overflows. Surely goodness and mercy and unfailing love shall follow me all the days of my life, And I shall dwell forever [throughout all my days] in the house and in the presence of the Lord.
~Psalm 23:1-6 (AMP)

Jesus, we ask that for every person reading this, You would fill them with the confidence that no matter what their path looks like or what obstacle is before them, You will never let go of their hand! We ask that you give them eyes to see with your perspective and that each one would trust your faithfulness to love them well. You are the Good Shepherd! You cause us to overcome every mountain! We love you, Lord. In Jesus' name, Amen.

ABOUT THE AUTHORS

Londa Harwell first experienced healing after suffering for many years with severe fibromyalgia and several other autoimmune diseases. In 2001, she was introduced to a method of inner healing. As her heart wounds healed, she also experienced a level of healing to her body, restoring her quality of life. In 2003, Londa became a facilitator for inner healing prayer ministry and later served as Director of Restoration Ministries at Voice Ministries for several years. She is an ordained pastor. She has spent thousands of hours in one-on-one prayer ministry. In 2014 through her years of experience in mind renewal and through the inspiration of Holy Spirit, she developed the method of mind renewal called the Value Exchange. Her passion is to come alongside people, helping them connect with the Lord in a way that brings relationship and helps them receive physical and emotional healing. Londa and her husband Christopher reside in Nappanee, Indiana, and have two daughters who have blessed them with several grand- and great-grandchildren.

· · · · ·

Starting in December of 2010, **Dr. Rachelle Crowder** suffered for 21 months with a bacterial infection called Clostridium Difficile (C-Diff). She almost died from the disease; however, in May of 2012 she was miraculously healed! Through that process she became exposed to the power of healing prayer. In 2012, Rachelle was introduced to inner healing when she met Londa Harwell. It wasn't long before a strong friendship formed. Rachelle began using the Value Exchange in her medical practice and witnessed many amazing emotional healings. She was amazed how quickly the Holy Spirit's voice can heal even deep heart wounds, which, in turn, helps the body to heal. She has been ministering in partnership with Londa since 2016. Rachelle and her husband Richard live in Goshen, Indiana, and have two children, a son and a daughter. Dr. Crowder started her family practice with Goshen Health System in the summer of 1999.

Made in the USA
Middletown, DE
10 May 2022

65583249R00117